Feb. 8/73

Happy Birthday
Sharon

love
Mom + Dad.

THE
SILENCE
OF THE
NORTH

THE SILENCE OF THE NORTH

by *Olive A. Fredrickson*
with Ben East

GENERAL PUBLISHING COMPANY LIMITED, TORONTO

Sections from Chapters 2, 4, 7, 8, 9, 10, 11, 12, 13, 14, 18, and 19 originally appeared in somewhat different form in *Outdoor Life* magazine under the following titles "I Had to Have Moose," copyright © 1967; "Wolves Were the Worst," copyright © 1967; "We Saw the Ice Go Out," copyright © 1969; "Starvation Wilderness," copyright © 1969; "Bears in My Hair," copyright © 1969; "Nightmare Spring," copyright © 1969. Popular Science Publishing Co. Used by permission.

Design by Iris Kleinman

Printed in the United States of America

For Olive and Vala,
who said so many times,
"Mom, you have a story to tell"

Contents

Illustrations facing page 108

Foreword

This story is true.

I think that is the most important thing to be said about it. The events and hardships recounted here may seem incredible to the reader, but they happened as they are told. I have known Olive Fredrickson for a number of years, have worked closely with her in the preparation of magazine stories as well as this book, and on that score I can say with assurance that there is not the slightest doubt. She remembers what took place and relates it as it happened.

Toward the end of summer in 1966, not too long after I had been named Senior Field Editor of *Outdoor Life* magazine, I was planning a trip to northern British Columbia, to spend a week or so at a remote fishing camp on Quesnel Lake near the town of Horsefly. Shortly before I was ready to leave, Bill Rae, my editor-in-chief, phoned me from New York. He had just received a lengthy manuscript from a woman living at Vanderhoof, some two hundred miles northwest of the place where I would be.

The writer recited a fantastic tale of privation and danger as a young widow on the frontier of northern Canada back in the 1930s. As the story stood, it was not right for *Outdoor Life*, but if we were to skim off the parts that fitted our requirements and do some further editorial work on them, Bill thought we would have a very exciting piece. Did I want to go to Vanderhoof and look into the possibilities?

I did, for two reasons. My work at that time consisted mostly of just that kind of research, along with the rewriting of material and some ghosting when it was necessary. In the second place, I was curious to meet this writer and I knew there would be a challenge in putting her story in shape.

That whole trip proved unusually interesting and fruitful. I tracked down and verified three authentic cases and one near-case of unprovoked cougar attack on humans, something that happens only rarely. I visited and obtained story material from a one-armed Indian guide who had been scalped by an enraged grizzly three years before. I flew to Lonesome Lake to get acquainted with Jack Turner and his wife and seven-year-old daughter, a family living on a homestead completely isolated in mountain wilderness, winter-feeding a flock of trumpeter swans under contract with the Canadian government, and hiking out once a month twenty-five miles to the nearest gravel road for their mail. Only the year before, Turner had killed a grizzly that was probably the largest ever shot in North America, dropping it at six feet when it came for him in an unprovoked and lightning-swift charge as he was walking a narrow trail along the Atnarko River.

Finally I drove north to Prince George, a bustling frontier town that still lacked sidewalks but where the guest of the week was the chairman of the board of the *London Times,* which was then opening a huge new paper mill there.

From Prince George I went on, in a cold September rain and plagued by a flat tire, to Vanderhoof to meet Olive Fredrickson and her husband, John.

They were living in a pleasant, meticulously neat house at the edge of town, with flowers in the yard, and the visit was a delight. I still have vivid memories of our noon meal that first day, with mashed potatoes and brown gravy that were unforgettable.

As for Olive herself, I had never met a more forthright and gracious woman. There was a simplicity and honesty about her that was irresistible.

Out of that visit came the material for two of the chapters of this book.

Bill Rae labeled "terrific" the stories I brought home from that trip, not the least so the Fredrickson pieces. When they were published, *Outdoor Life* readers agreed.

The magazine ran a two-part series in the summer of 1967. About the time it appeared we received a second long manuscript from Olive, which formed the basis of three additional tales that we used in 1969.

Seldom has *Outdoor Life* carried any story that evoked such astonishing reader response. Letters poured in to the editorial office and to Olive herself from every part of the United States and Canada. Typical was the comment from a woman in upstate New York, who wrote, "These are the two most wonderful stories I have ever read. What a remarkable woman!"

Bill Rae once commented that Olive Fredrickson is so full of surprises that you can expect anything. But she has two qualities that never falter—her courage and her basic honesty. When her eyesight began to fail a year ago and she was told that ultimately she faced total blindness, she wrote me simply, "My hart is broke, of course, but I've had hartbrakes before."

Another attribute she has is total recall, even of events that happened sixty years ago.

Her lack of formal schooling—she grew up forty-five miles from the nearest school—reveals itself in one way, a highly original style of spelling. Even there, while she is creating her own word forms as they sound to her, she abides by certain rules of logic and common sense.

"Choose" becomes "chuse," "heartbreak" is "hartbrake," "accident" turns into "axedent," "certainly" comes out as "sertinly."

It's unique, but it is not difficult to read and it even adds a quaint charm to her straightforward prose. I have not known anyone to whom Olive's spelling has come who has not enjoyed it.

I know no better way to portray the innocence, and also the warmth and sincerity, of this unusual pioneer woman than by quoting the sentence with which she ended her own version of this story, before it was edited.

"If anyone who reads this story wants to come and see us and talk about the country, the wild animals and their ways, and the experiences we have had, we will tell truthfully all we know about it, and tell it with pleasure," she wrote.

It was an invitation she meant.

If I have served her as well as she deserves in the pages that follow, I am proud to have had the opportunity.

BEN EAST
Holly, Michigan
January 1, 1972

1

The House of Sadness

The first gray light of morning was staining the windows of the house when the child awoke. The pale, worn woman in the bed beside her was trembling and making queer moaning sounds.

The girl sat up and rubbed the sleep from her eyes. She saw then that there was thin foam on the woman's lips, flecked red with blood. The child was only nine, but she had had enough to do with caring for an epileptic to know what was needed. She scrambled off the bed and ran to the kitchen for a spoon to hold down the stricken woman's tongue, safely out of the way of the teeth that ground together as the sunken jaws worked spasmodically.

The moaning noise had ceased when she got back to the bed, and the woman was lying very still. An older sister and brother were sleeping in the loft above, and the girl called now, in fright: "Come down here. Hurry, Mama is having a hard spell."

Maud, the sister, was first to come flying down the stairs. She laid a hand on the woman's chest, waited a moment in silence, then choked out three words. "She's dead, Alta," she told the child.

I was that child—Alta Goodwin, nine years old, motherless.

My memory of the house where it happened has dimmed with the passage of time, but there were some things about it that still stand clear and distinct in my mind, and I still think of it as a house of sadness, more than sixty years later. Mother died on December 1, 1910.

The house was built of logs, with a single room downstairs, the kitchen in one corner, and makeshift bedrooms above. It stood on the low bank of the Sturgeon River, near what is now the town of Gibbons, about twenty-five miles northeast of Edmonton, with the level grain fields of the Alberta prairie running off to the horizon on all sides.

The place belonged to Joe McLean, who ran a store, post office and eating place in a low-roofed log building on the old Athabasca Landing Trail, a mile or two farther down the Sturgeon, near the place called the Elbow, where the river doubled back to the southeast to run into the North Saskatchewan.

The house was small and bleak, but we rented it from McLean and it was certainly worth more than we paid him. I never knew what became of the money my father got from the sale of our home in Wisconsin. I was told it brought $4,500, and at the time that was a considerable sum. But I suppose the long move to Alberta was expensive, and the money apparently was gone before mother died. Shortly before her death I recall her telling one of the boys, "The rent is due again. You go and see McLean and tell him that your father is still away and we don't have the money."

The message that came back was, "That's all right, Mrs. Goodwin. You can pay me when your husband gets home in the spring. Don't worry about it."

The sparsely settled North had many people as generous and kind as that in those days.

The furnishings of the house were plain, mostly rude by today's standards, but we did have a few good pieces, left over from better days. The kitchen stove burned wood and had a warming oven above and a water reservoir at one end. There were two small hinged shelves at the back that could be lowered close to the cooking lids, and these were ideal for keeping a stack of pancakes hot.

I remember vividly Mother's big rocking chair, covered with an afghan she had knitted, in pink, blue, black, and yellow. There was a heavy oak table, round and big enough for our family of fourteen to sit around at one time. Between meals it was kept covered with a white oilcloth and set with a sugar bowl, spoon holder, and a few other pieces in the center.

The outstanding item in the house was an old-fashioned organ, beautifully carved. Mother loved music, especially the oldtime favorites and certain hymns. I can still hear my sister Maud playing and singing for her, "Rock of Ages," "Home, Sweet Home," "Annie Laurie," and "When the Roll Is Called Up Yonder."

We had brought the organ and the big table with us when we moved to Edmonton from Wisconsin in the spring of 1909. When we moved on after Mother's death they were left behind, along with the remaining few of her prized possessions that had survived the long trip from Wisconsin. Someone has commented that the settling of the American West was harder on the pioneer women than on the men who drove the wagon trains. Certainly that was true in the North of western Canada.

In the summer of 1910, not too long before Mother died, my father and three of my brothers (I was the youngest of twelve children), Elmer, Menzo and Willie, had gone north to Lesser Slave Lake for the winter, with Willie's wife, Maggie. They wanted to look over the country in the hope of finding a place where they could homestead in good fur country and live off the land.

I was left alone with Mother for a time. I couldn't go to school, for she was not well enough to be left by herself. She had brought four girls and eight boys into the world and raised them, and her strength and health were gone. Finally, acute epilepsy made it necessary for someone to be with her at all times. Her seizures were severe and frequent, and I am sure now that she realized her life was nearing its end.

Archie Goodwin, my father, is remembered by Hugh Neff, a former neighbor, as "probably the greatest hunter and pioneer that ever lived in Clark County, Wisconsin. In those days, before the turn of the century, there were still a few panthers in this state. As a boy, I remember my father telling us about finding a deer that had been killed near Black River, partly eaten, and the remains covered with leaves and litter. Goodwin climbed up in a tree, kept watch until the killer returned to finish the deer and shot one of the last panthers killed in Wisconsin. Another time a lumber company raising their own beef cattle near Stanley found two or three steers killed, with their throats cut. The company people did nothing about the loss, believing it was the work of some disgruntled employee who had been fired and was out to get revenge. But when word of the occurrence reached Goodwin, he had other ideas. He went to the place where the company had the steers in a corral, sat up and watched, and bagged another panther."

That was one side of our father, the admirable side. A great hunter and trapper, a born pioneer, loving the wilderness and moving on with it as it receded. Unfortunately there was another side.

Long ago I was forced to the conclusion that he sold out in the States and sought new, wild land in Canada mainly for one compelling reason: he was a heavy drinker, and when he was drunk, his temper, always hair-triggered and formidable, was as foul as any I have ever known.

He'd come home and beat Mother and any of the children he could lay hands on. We endured cruel whippings and actual beatings that were entirely undeserved, not once but many times. I'll never forget those unhappy occasions and my heartbreak at being punished for something I was not guilty of.

Father was a good man when it came to honesty. He was hard-working and neighborly and well respected in the places where he lived. But he was never a kind man to his wife and children. In the latter years of his life he quit drinking altogether which made things better, but we still had to live with that quick, fiendish temper.

My brothers Rollo and Lea were still at home when Dad left for Lesser Slave with three of the older boys, but it was decided that they should go to school while I stayed home with Mother. I guess the theory was that, as the youngest child, I'd have plenty of time for school later on. Unhappily, things never worked out that way.

Mother failed steadily through the fall. Looking back across the years, I can see plenty of evidence that she knew her days were numbered.

Lea and Rollo did most of the cooking, but she started teaching me more about it, even showing me how to mix and bake bread. She also taught me to sew, to patch and mend rips in our clothing, and she began to teach me to knit socks and mittens.

I enjoyed learning these things. I had been by myself a great deal while the boys were at school, with no playmate nearby, and the lessons gave me something to do. I even took over the family washing, doing it on an old-fashioned washboard, and learned to iron the clothes with the heavy irons that were heated on top of the wood stove.

Mother had long serious talks with the three of us, reading from the Bible, warning us against the evils of drinking and gambling, and urging us to be ready to look after ourselves if she failed to come out of one of her "sick spells," as we called her seizures. I remember crying for a long time after those talks.

We knew far less about epilepsy in those days than is known now, and the seizures were terrifying things for a young child to watch. Mother's were severe in the extreme, for she was a victim of the form known as grand mal. When an attack came she fell heavily wherever she was.

I recall one time in particular, in the early fall of 1910. We got our drinking water from a lovely spring not far from the house, and I had gone for a bucketful. I loitered, something I did very rarely. There were sheep grazing near the spring and a few frisky lambs playing on a cut bank. I stopped to watch them.

By that time Mother was becoming increasingly nervous, suffering from an obsessive fear that someone was out to hurt her or her children. She'd sit each afternoon watching the road where Lea and Rollo would come from school, keeping me close beside her, and when she finally saw them coming she'd breathe out a long sigh and whisper a fervent "Thank God!" Her sense of relief from imagined danger at such times was pitiable.

She grew worried about me while I was watching the lambs and came to look for me. I saw her coming, and then she fell suddenly and lay shaking and twitching on the ground. When I reached her, froth and blood were oozing from her mouth.

I ran to the house for a spoon and forced it between her clenched teeth. Unconscious, she had already bitten her tongue cruelly; she wore an upper denture, and it had dropped back into her throat and was threatening to strangle her. She bit me hard when I tried to get it out, but I finally succeeded, got her tongue depressed, and knelt beside her and waited for the seizure to pass. When she regained consciousness she lay and rested for a time, then I helped her to her feet, we made our way slowly to the house, and she lay down on her bed.

I cried for hours. My sister Maud had married and left home some time before, but her husband, Gene McHugh, did not have steady work, and I begged mother to write and ask the two of them to come and stay with us. I couldn't endure the thought of being alone with her any longer.

Maud replied at once, saying they would come, and a few days later they arrived. I recall that as one of the few happy days of that terribly long summer and fall. Not only was there someone at hand now to take care of our mother, but in a secret place in my mind I was cherishing a small dream of my own. If Maud and Gene stayed long enough, I could go to school.

Maud made me a couple of gingham dresses, the first new clothes I had had in a long time, and the dream and my pride began to grow. Finally the plans were talked of openly. I'd start school very soon.

But then the bubble burst. Maud's husband and my brother Rollo decided to trap muskrats at a place called Two Lakes, thirty miles north of our home. Lea quit school and went to work for Joe McLean, to get money we needed so badly. It was too far for me to walk to school alone, and my dream ended in tears.

Maud and I were alone with Mother by day. Lea came home to spend the nights.

About that time, when the family was together one Sunday, we decided to give Mother a special treat. She had not been out of the house for many weeks, except to go to the outside toilet. She had always loved the outdoors and everything in it, always had a few wild animals and birds tame enough to follow her around and eat from her hands. We knew how much she had missed seeing the countryside, so we borrowed a team of small, gentle horses and an old wagon and made plans to take her for a ride. Lea was only thirteen, but could handle horses well.

We laid a plank across the wagon box for a seat, put mother's rocking chair in the back and helped her in. Then we drove a couple of miles at a slow, safe walk, and she was enjoying everything as much as a child seeing it all for the first time. At the schoolhouse where Lea and Rollo had attended school we turned around and started home. It had been a fine Sunday drive.

We had only a short distance to go to the house when disaster struck. Mother's rocker had shifted slowly to one side. Now one of the rockers dropped into a crack in the wagon box and the chair tipped, pitching her to the ground.

She cried out and caught at the side of the box with one hand as she fell. Lea shouted "Whoa!" and the team stopped in its tracks, but a hind wheel of the wagon had run angling across Mother's chest.

Lea and Rollo helped her to her feet and walked her slowly the rest of the way to the house. When they got her into bed she bit her lips in pain until they bled, and although she told us she was not badly hurt, her strength failed steadily after that. In a few more weeks she was dead.

I was not allowed to go with the rest of the family to the small churchyard where she was buried. I suppose the others thought it would be too much for me. Neighbors came and laid her out on a cot in the downstairs room. A team and sleigh brought a coffin from Edmonton, and Lea borrowed a team and drove to Two Lakes to bring Rollo and Maud's husband home for the funeral. I remember little of it, and then another team and sleigh took her away, to a cemetery at a place called Sunnyside.

More than fifty years afterward I went to visit my brother John near Edmonton, and he took me to the spot where Mother had been buried. The church was gone, and the little cemetery of about a dozen graves had disappeared under a farmer's plow.

When that part of Canada was surveyed, sometime before 1900, it was laid out in square miles. Often the newly established section lines did not coincide with the early trails, churches, and other landmarks, and in many cases the latter were gradually abandoned and became grain fields.

It is only natural that it should happen that way. Nevertheless, in the case of our mother it seemed like a sad and undeserved final indignity for a woman who had undergone so much and to whom life had been so niggardly with even its small pleasures. I still grieve when I think of the bronze wheat ripening over that unmarked grave.

2

North to the Peace

There was no railroad north of Edmonton in 1910, and the road beyond Athabasca Landing was almost impossible to travel in summer. We had no quick way to send word to our father and the three boys that mother had died, even if we had known their exact whereabouts, which we didn't.

Maud and her husband stayed on with me. It was almost five months before father got a message from the Royal Canadian Mounted Police, telling him that his wife was dead.

Then it took the four men and Willie's wife, Maggie, another month to come the one hundred and eighty miles home, following the old Klondike Gold Trail by team and wagon, through muskeg so bad that some days they did well to make two miles, with mosquitoes and blackflies making both the days and nights an agony.

In dozens of places they had to cut trees and build corduroy across the worst of the muskeg, and the wagons were unloaded and reloaded many times a day.

They reached the home place in May. Father seemed to waste

little time in grieving for his dead wife. Almost the first thing he said to us was, "We're going to move north to the Peace River country. We'll start as soon as we can get packed."

Maud and her husband left to go back across the border to the United States, to find work and live. I wanted to go with them but Father said no, he'd take me north with him and the boys.

We left in late June with two teams and wagons, taking all the possessions the wagons would hold, including a crate of ten chickens. There was no room for the organ and the big oak table that Mother had loved so dearly, I suppose because they served to remind her of the better life that had been left behind in Wisconsin. But there wouldn't be much use for an organ on the frontier, where we were headed, and we could build a table when we got there. And with Mother six months in an unmarked grave, it didn't seem to matter greatly, even to me, whether these things went with us or not.

My brothers and I packed and took along a few old school books. I was still determined to get a little education if I could.

We never got to the Peace.

My brother Elmer wasn't with us. He had taken a job driving the stagecoach from Edmonton to Athabasca Landing, hauling passengers and mail. At our first camping place, at the Vermilion River, sitting around an open fire, we watched him trot smartly past, on the box of the same kind of oldtime stage seen today in western movies and television shows.

At Athabasca Landing his mail and passengers would be transferred onto a stern-wheeler, the *Northern Echo*, to continue either up or down the Athabasca River. Both ways, the mile-wide Athabasca was plagued with dangerous rapids, and both travel and freighting were beset with difficulty.

Upstream, the *Northern Echo* could go as far as Smith Landing. From there a stagecoach and horse-drawn wagons took over, carrying people, mail, and freight on to Peace River Crossing, Grande Prairie, and Fort St. John in British Columbia.

From Athabasca Landing downriver the going was all by water, and even harder. A steamboat, the *Northern Star,* went down the river to the head of fast water at Grand Rapids. There everything was loaded onto big scows and rolled across a half mile of land on wooden rollers. A dozen men teamed up on a line could pull a heavily loaded scow. Below the rapids the scows were floated and the journey continued, with freight, passengers, and mail aboard.

A good river man could run the remaining rapids as far down as Fort McMurray. There another steamboat took over for the remainder of the trip to Lake Athabasca and Fort Chipewyan.

Looking back, I still marvel at the skill and daring of the men who ran those river steamboats. The one I remember best was Joe Bird, a big, dark-skinned, eagle-eyed man with whom, a few years later, I would make one of the most dangerous and frightening trips of my life. In 1910 he was captain of the *Northern Echo.* He and Moses Leveque, a French Canadian who was first mate on the *Northern Star,* hauled mail on the Athabasca by horse team and sleigh in winter. They knew the river and its danger spots at all seasons as most of us know our front yards.

The mail that went down north from Fort McMurray in winter was carried by dog team, and later my brother Frank drove one of these teams part of the way.

The Athabasca Landing Trail, as the stage-and-freight road north to the Landing was called, was a good road by the standards of that day, and we made good time that far, although there were ruts and mudholes to contend with.

Athabasca Landing was a rather drab-looking frontier settlement in the summer of 1911, despite the fact that it was maybe the most important freighting center in the North of Canada. It consisted of a huddle of thirty or forty houses, Hudson's Bay Company buildings, and big sheds that served as warehouses, strung along the low bank of the river, with streets that could be ankle deep in dust one day, knee deep in mud the next.

All the goods for the trading posts and the growing settlements farther north went by way of Edmonton and were freighted north over the Trail to the Landing, to be shipped on by steamboat. In the gold rush of 1897 and 1898 hundreds of gold-hungry travelers had passed through the Landing, headed up the same Klondike Trail we intended to follow. And in the years after that hundreds more homesteaders like ourselves came that same way, seeking land in the Peace River country. Much of the color and action came to an end, however, in 1912, when the railroad from Edmonton reached the Landing.

To a girl not yet ten years old, accustomed to the isolation and loneliness of the log house back on the Sturgeon, it was an exciting and romantic place. I imagined it a real city, and reveled in the sights and sounds of it every minute. There were stagecoaches and freight wagons arriving and leaving, loading and unloading. The biggest event of all was the stern-wheeler *Northern Echo* rounding a bend with a hoarse blast of her whistle, and nosing in to the bank to tie up. All told, I was sorry when the time came to leave.

We had camped there for five days, resting our teams and ourselves, when on a fine morning in mid-July we crossed the river on a ferry scow and headed north on the old Klondike Gold Trail.

There was no wagon road on the west side of the Athabasca, and to this day I do not know the reason. The land there was sandy and firm, and it still seems to me that the early travelers could have punched a road north along that bank far more easily than on the east side, where the Klondike Trail ran through all but impassable muskeg.

For the first nine miles north of the Landing we had no trouble.

The road was fairly good and we passed a few farms. I still remember the black, rich-looking earth and the oats and wheat, nearly as tall as the fenceposts, waving in the summer wind.

We camped under the stars at night. The weather was fine and there was no need to put up a tent. So far, I was finding our long move north a pleasant childhood adventure.

My brothers and I had been given ten chickens by a neighbor back on the Sturgeon, in return for taking care of chicks. They were the first live playthings we had had since leaving Wisconsin, and we loved them and had made pets of them. At our camps we let them out of their crate, fed and watered them, and cleaned the crate. They stayed close by us, and young as I was, they helped me to feel that this new country we were going to was going to be home.

It is hard to describe the beauty of those first few campsites along the Klondike Trail. They were old campgrounds used by a great many people, some on their way to Dawson City and the goldfields, others leaving civilization to take their pick of the fertile farmlands along the Peace. Those early pioneers must have chosen their overnight stopping places because they looked good, as well as for the horse feed and water they offered. They were timbered, had plenty of grass, and small clear streams veined them.

We made camp one night at a place called Jackknife. A man had been killed there in a knife fight some years before. The man who did the killing claimed to have acted in self-defense and he was still there, putting up freight teams overnight in winter for a dollar a team.

Beyond Jackknife we plunged into muskeg country that beggars description, and was harder on stock than on people. We felled trees, built pole bridges over the creeks, and laid corduroy in the mudholes.

At many of the creek crossings we saw the remains of horses

and oxen half sunk in the mud. Some had been there for years and only a few bones were left. Other carcasses were still covered with dried hide. The mosquitoes, horseflies, blackflies, deer flies, and bot flies, coupled with hoof rot and a disease the pioneers called swamp fever, had been too much for the poor brutes. I suppose most of them had gotten stuck in the muskeg, were too weakened to get out, and died under the terrible insect attacks. I saw those dead animals more than sixty years ago but I still don't like to think about them.

Father had bought small, tough horses in Edmonton for the trip, the kind that were locally and somewhat derisively known as broomtails. They weighed nine hundred to twelve hundred pounds, and he had been told that they would endure flies, hoof rot, and swamp fever better than larger animals.

Many times I saw a horse driven almost insane by the flies, rearing, kicking, pawing the air, trying to run away. We took the best care of them we could, washing the mud from their feet, legs, and bellies each night and sponging the tops of their necks and shoulders to prevent the collars from galling.

In the first week out of Athabasca Landing we made only twenty-nine miles. At that rate winter would overtake us long before we reached the Peace River country.

The grown-ups were worried and tired out night after night, but Rollo and Lea and I were having the time of our lives. We went barefoot since it was better to wade through the mud and water of the muskeg that way. But there was frost just under the moss, and although it was only early August, the nights were turning chill. For the first hour or two in the morning our feet ached with cold, but we accepted that as part of the adventure.

I was amusing myself with the things a small girl could be expected to do. I soon learned that in a single evening I could coax the gray jays, the whiskeyjacks that are so common in the North of Canada, up close enough that a few of them would feed from my hand. Bluejays and chickadees came around for a snack whenever we fed our chickens, and although they were never as tame and bold as the gray jays, they furnished a lot of entertainment.

We came to a place called Whiskey Plains, and from the top of a low hill where we ate our noon meal we counted twenty-one horses that had died within the last month or two. The pioneers in the Peace and Athabasca River valleys paid dear for their new homes, and nowhere was the price more evident than in the string of dead stock along the Klondike Trail.

Time after time we found wry and bitter comments recorded in brief messages carved in the bark of trees or on boards nailed to the trunks. Some of the travelers with more imagination (or more hardship) than others had decorated their notices with devil faces. Others had contented themselves with giving the place a name and recording it for those who would follow. There were places called Hells Hole, Devils Canyon, Dead Horse Valley, and Killer Muskeg.

One of the most eloquent signs we encountered read, "You're Dead If You Go Ahead." Another was hand-lettered on two boards nailed to trees a mile apart. The first proclaimed boldly, "Dawson City or Bust!" A mile farther on the rest of the story was recorded in one word, "Busted!" in big letters. It was easy to imagine the gold seeker leaving his team dead in the muskeg, packing a blanket and a little grub on his back and pushing doggedly on on foot. Many did it that way.

At the place called Hells Hole, Father was digging a shallow trench around our campfire to make sure the fire did not spread into the moss and leaves and dry stuff. He scraped away a shovelful of litter and turned up a human kneecap and part of the bones of a leg and foot. We heard him mutter under his breath.

He covered the bones carefully and chose another spot for our fire. We never learned the story of those bones and that lonely shallow grave, but it was easy to picture the man dying on the trail, back in the gold-rush days, and being buried at the campsite because there was nothing else for his companions to do. Nobody would pack a body out from such a spot as that just for the sake of burying it in a cemetery. And if the time was winter, when the earth was iron hard, the grave would have been no more than a scooped-out hollow in the snow.

Bones of men and bones of horses, mileposts on that terrible trail!

Our teams were suffering more and more from the flies. We contrived head nets to protect their ears, and where the insect bites left raw sores on their chins, necks, and down the inside of their legs we smeared them with wagon grease to keep the pests off. Our own bites were almost as bad, but the leftover fat from fried salt pork made a pretty good repellent.

Two days after Father had unearthed the human bones, we camped beside one of the worst mudholes we had seen. The muskeg stretched ahead as far as we could see, and there were a dozen wagon tracks fanning out across it, where traveler after traveler had tried to find a route of his own across.

Many had not made it. The sorry remains of wagons were sticking out of the mud, some with a wheel missing, others with tongue or box broken. And again the skeletons of horses and oxen were scattered along the tracks.

Some showed only a hoof and leg, others horns or ears. We saw the bones of one poor horse that lay arched up like a bow. Its teammate must have pushed its head down in the mud as they struggled to regain their footing and it had died in that position.

Nothing we had seen on the whole trip was more discouraging than that stretch of muskeg with its grim relics.

"Nobody should try to travel this God-forsaken trail in summer," Pa admitted to the boys around the fire that night. We knew he was right. In the fall when the muskeg was frozen and the heavy snow had not yet come, and again in spring after most of the snow was gone, wagons could make out. In summer, when we had chosen to risk the trip, it was a question whether anybody would get through.

Father and the boys cut trees and built corduroy across that whole mudhole and we crossed it without mishap, maybe in part because our wagons were not too heavily loaded now, after almost two months of travel.

We had started with only a bare minimum of supplies, flour, beans, rice, cornmeal and oatmeal, tea, salt pork, and dried apples. We also had sugar and a few odds and ends of dried vegetables. Our meals in camp had cut heavily into these stores and at this point we were traveling light.

The night after we crossed the bad muskeg a thin skim of ice froze on the water puddles. Time was running out on us and it seemed less and less likely that we could make it to our destination before the onset of winter.

The next day the road ran for almost ten miles along ridges studded with aspen and jackpine, and for the first time in many days we made good time. About five o'clock that evening we topped a ridge and broke clear of the timber, to gaze out over some of the nicest hay meadows we had ever seen.

At the foot of the slope we came to a beautiful clear stream about ten feet wide. A sign nailed to a tree said "Tomato Creek."

"Whoever named it had a big imagination," I heard Rollo tell Lea.

We never knew how the place got its name. You could no more grow tomatoes there than on the moon. In shady places there was frost a foot down in the muskeg all summer, and there were few nights even in July and August when water didn't freeze in the shallow pools. But if it couldn't grow tomatoes, it at least had an abundance of the kind of horse feed every team driver dreams about, and it was as pretty a spot as I have ever seen anywhere in the North.

Hay grew rank and thick in every meadow. It was not the common slough grass that we had seen in the muskeg all the way along. Our horses had done only moderately well on that. Nor was this bluejoint or redtop, with which we were familiar. It grew only about two feet tall, and while I'm still not sure, I believe it was the famous short grass of the buffalo prairies. Our horses thrived on it.

Dad and the boys put up a good camp in a small sheltered opening a short distance from the creek, and I decided that they intended to stay here for quite some time. I didn't dream how long.

A day later, when everything in camp was snug, they went up and down the creek exploring. The meadowland was far more extensive than they had guessed. It seemed to reach everywhere. And where aspen ridges cut across the meadows, the ground was covered to the height of a horse's belly with thick pea vine and vetch, equally good horse feed.

This was virgin country, lush and verdant and beautiful, a land of incredible abundance, unmarked by so much as a single wagon track, ready and waiting for the ax and the settler's plow. It did not take Father long to decide that he had found what he was seeking, even though we were still many miles south of the Peace.

The supply of wild food for humans was almost as plentiful as for livestock. Moose tracks were all around and rabbits were almost as thick as flies. Wherever there was open pine timber the ground was carpeted with blueberries, and the bogs held far more cranberries than we could possibly pick.

None of us was surprised when father told us, beside the fire the second evening, "We'll winter here. It's getting late in the year, and we've just got time to put up hay for our horses."

The next day he and the boys went hunting. Half a mile from

camp John downed a bull moose, rolling fat and with a rack of antlers so wide that his old long-barreled British .303 could not quite reach across them.

It had been a long time since we had tasted fresh meat and that moose was a real windfall. My sister-in-law Maggie, Willie's wife, and I started in right after breakfast the next morning to dry the meat. We cut it in thin strips, hung them on a pole rack, and kept a smoky fire of green wood going underneath to keep blowflies off and smoke the meat as it dried. Moose jerky made that way turns as hard and dry as a piece of weathered driftwood, but it is tasty and about as nourishing, ounce for ounce, as any meat a man will ever find. I have known north-country trappers who carried a strip of it on their trapline and made a very satisfactory noon meal by whacking off a small chunk and chewing on it as they walked.

We had brought scythes, and Dad and the boys started in at once to mow hay. For the first day or two we could hear the rhythmic swishing of the scythes and the singsong strokes of the whetstones as they were laid against the blades, first on one side, then on the other. It was a pleasant sound and it made camp seem more like a real home. But then they moved farther away and we could no longer hear them work.

When Maggie and I finished our camp chores we built up the smoke fire under the moose meat and went picking blueberries and cranberries. We dried them by the pailful on a piece of canvas spread out in the sun, put them in empty flour sacks, and hung them on the ridgepole in one of the tents.

I still remember the day Rollo decided to trap a bear. He set the trap about a mile from camp, and the next morning he invited me to go with him to look at it. He had had no luck with the bear, but he had caught a big skunk. We shot it, pried the trap jaws apart with clamps, and put our catch in a packsack. Rollo carried it back to camp over his shoulder.

On Pa's emphatic orders we stripped, took a bath in the creek, and buried the offending clothes in moss for a few days. But we also skinned the skunk and stretched the pelt, and it finally brought two dollars.

"Next time you catch one of them, drag it home with a string," Father ordered sternly. It was one piece of advice from him that I still regard as very sound.

The work of cutting hay for winter horse feed kept all of us busy as fall came on. By the middle of September the grass started to turn yellow, and we hurried to finish the job.

Father made hand rakes for all of us by boring holes an inch or two apart in a flat piece of wood with an auger, fitting pegs the size of a man's finger for teeth, and adding a long smooth pole for a handle. We raked the sun-dried hay into piles. Then, by shoving two slim poles under each pile, with a person at each end of the poles, we could pick up the load and carry it to a stack.

Where the meadows were dry and firm enough to hold up a team and wagon we speeded up the work by hauling the hay to the stack on a homemade rack. But most of it was gathered by hand. Long before the first snowfall we had enough to see our teams through until the wild pastures turned green again in the spring. My brother John told me years later that we put up ninety tons of hay that summer and fall, all of it with scythes and hand rakes.

When the haying was finished we moved a mile or two down Tomato Creek, to a better campsite on an open aspen flat, and put up the tents again.

We had not made it to the Peace River valley, as we had planned back on the Sturgeon. But we had found a new home in beautiful country, and nobody seemed to think the change in plans mattered.

3

Goodwin's Halfway House

We knew the winter would bring heavy snow and severe cold. As soon as haying was ended, Father and the boys began work on a log house, and shortly before Christmas we moved in.

The house building had been delayed, first by haying in the early fall, then by the trapping Father and the boys did while they went ahead with the work of cutting and fitting the logs.

By Christmas the weather had turned very cold. I still remember a night when the thermometer went down to 31 degrees below zero. Our tents didn't hold heat well, and we were sleeping with all our clothes on, as many to a bed as could crowd in, to keep each other warm. The solid walls of the house, chinked and windproof, were a welcome change.

It had only one room, with two small windows and a door at the south end. The floor was packed earth, and there was no fireplace and no real chimney at first.

The room was large, twenty-two by twenty-four feet. We built our fire on the dirt floor, Indian fashion, cut a hole in the pole roof directly above it and fashioned a sort of stack of poles over the hole, about three feet high, to get more draft and help pull the smoke out. Most of the time this crude system worked well enough. The smoke from the open fire eddied slowly toward the roof, vanished up the stack and was gone. But if the wind blew from the wrong direction or atmospheric conditions were wrong, we huddled around the fire, rubbing our eyes, half suffocated.

We built bunks along the back wall, one above another, and made mattresses for them by sewing grain sacks together and stuffing them with dry hay. They were soft and comfortable but not warm. Before the winter was over we solved that by putting a dried moose hide under each mattress. That shut out the cold that had come up from the bottom and left us shivering in bed so many nights.

Before the winter was far along, Dad and Rollo went on a trip to look over the country to the west of us. Somewhat to their surprise, they found that the Athabasca River was only about three miles from the place where we were living. There was a well-traveled road on the river ice, packed hard by freight teams. There was also a much-used campground on the bank, sheltered in an open stand of spruce and pine, and it was plain that a great many teams had been tied to the trees there for a night.

Father came back from that trip fired up with an idea. We would build log barns and a log bunkhouse at that campground, and put up teams and people overnight.

The work was begun at once, and before spring we had a makeshift bunkhouse and barns finished, with dirt floors and pole roofs covered with hay. And almost before the buildings were ready the bunkhouse was filled with people night after night and the barns with horses, mules, and oxen.

The campground was about halfway between the place we called Jackknife and another, farther up the Athabasca, known as Fish Camp, so it naturally took the name of Goodwin's Halfway House. It was about a fifteen-mile drive either way to the other camps, a good day of travel for a heavily loaded team even on the river ice, and the Halfway House quickly became one of the busiest and most popular stopover places along the river. Before we were through I saw sixty teams tied and fed in our barns in a single night.

The first thing we needed, as we went ahead with the work of putting up the log buildings, was two sleighs for hauling hay and supplies down to the river site from Tomato Creek. We did not have a nail, spike, or bolt to work with, but our father was the kind of pioneer who knew how to improvise and was skilled with the tools of the frontier, ax, broadax, saw, and auger.

He started planning the sleighs in the early fall, cutting birch logs for the runners, bunk, and bolsters, and pine poles for the rack. Each piece was peeled and hewed into shape and then racked in the sun to season and dry, for the sake of lightness.

The runners were birch logs, chosen for a natural curve at the front end, and hewed smooth on the sides and top but with only the bark removed on the bottom, so that the hard, rounded wood would harden with use.

Everything was fitted together by notching, boring holes, and driving stout wooden pins in place. When the job was finished we had two sleighs as sturdy and usable as anything ever turned out by a factory, without an ounce of iron in them anywhere. They were ready by the time the barns were built, and Lea, John, and Willie started daily trips, hauling hay down from the home place to the Halfway House. Menzo and Rollo stayed there, feeding and caring for the teams.

Father charged a dollar a night for a team. I do not remember what the freighters themselves paid to sleep in the bunkhouse, but I know the Goodwin family was finally engaged in a profitable business. The Hudson's Bay and Northwest Trading companies each had about sixteen freight teams on the river, and the mail team also went past our place. There was never a dull minute.

Meanwhile, back at the house on Tomato Creek we were having trouble with a leaky roof. When the snow started to thaw in the early spring, water ran through in streams. We knew that as soon as the sap started to rise in the birch trees their bark would peel easily. When the time came, Father felled tree after tree and cut a ring around the trunks every three feet. He was able to peel the bark off in slabs that were three feet long and averaged two to three feet wide. He laid those slabs on the roof like shingles, peeled side up, until the roof was covered, adding poles to hold the slabs flat. But they quickly curled in the spring sun, and the roof leaked as badly as before.

Next Father ordered a whipsaw brought up from Athabasca Landing, and he and the boys whipsawed lumber for a permanent roof. With tar paper and some hay between the boards, that roof lasted for nine years.

Next came a rough board floor in the home place and in the bunkhouse at the river. Things were getting better all the time, and by the fall of 1912, when we had been there a year, we had it pretty comfortable and were making money in earnest.

In spite of all the work, Dad had found time to do some trapping the first winter. His heart was always in this, and he was good at it. Fox and lynx sign was plentiful, and the trapline yielded a good catch of fur before spring.

There was never any scarcity of meat, for moose, deer, and caribou roamed the wild country around us.

In the spring, when the river ice was no longer safe to travel, the teams came past Tomato Creek until the rutted wagon road thawed and became a quagmire of mud. Then the ice went out, and freight, mail, and passengers traveled the Athabasca by steamboat once more.

A homesteader going north that spring sold us a cow for one hundred dollars. She was about to drop a calf, and he realized he might lose both the cow and calf if he continued to lead her behind his wagon. Two days after we acquired her, she presented us with a fine heifer calf. She was our first cow, the beginning of a herd of cattle that would finally number more than fifty. She was gentle and docile but hard to milk, and I was never able to milk her. That chore went to one or another of the boys.

Rollo and I had made a little money around the barns and bunkhouse by brushing and currying freight teams and washing dishes for travelers. Whenever a homesteader came by with chickens we tried to buy a few with that money, and gradually our flock grew.

The nearest schoolhouse was forty-five miles away, and I gave up all hope of ever attending school. I began studying in the old schoolbooks we had brought north, whenever I could find a bit of spare time, which wasn't often.

My brother Elmer came home from his job of driving the stage-coach, and we all settled down to putting up hay, running trap-lines, and managing the Halfway House.

As soon as freeze-up came in the fall of 1912, Father and John went back to the settlements north of Edmonton and brought home factory bobsleds loaded with foodstuff, nails, spikes, building paper, and the other supplies we needed so badly. Next, they turned their attention to trapping muskrats, foxes, weasels, mink, and lynx.

At that point a profitable sideline to the trapping turned up. Fox ranching was beginning to be a fast-growing industry in Canada, and there was a brisk market for breeding stock, with fantastically high prices paid for blacks and silvers. My brothers built a big pen, and if they caught a black or silver that was not badly injured in the trap, it went into that pen for later sale. By spring in 1913 we had two beautiful silver foxes and one black, and in May one of the silvers had a litter of four pups.

That gave Rollo the idea of capturing live fox pups for sale, from wild dens. He and Elmer started den hunting and struck it rich the second day. They found a den on a timbered ridge about three miles up Tomato Creek from our house, and when they dug it out they were rewarded with a female silver and a male black pup.

We named them Fluff and Pedro and made pets of them. Before the summer was over the boys sold them to a fur buyer for $1,700. He told us he intended to take them to Prince Edward Island as a start toward a fox farm.

We raised quite a number of foxes ourselves from then on, and the boys continued den hunting with fair success. The lowest price we ever got for a live animal was two hundred dollars. But in 1918 the fox-ranching bubble burst and prices plummeted. That ended the best of the fox business.

About 1916 the railroad from Athabasca Landing reached the Peace River and Dawson Creek. It had been built from Edmonton north to the Landing a few years earlier, I believe in 1912. Its completion sounded the death knell of freighting by steamboat and horse teams on the Athabasca. It also ended the flow of people and supplies past our place, and Goodwin's Halfway House went out of business.

We were cut off from the outside world almost completely now, save for the once-a-year trip Father and the boys made back to the settlements for supplies. Between those trips our telegraph linemen, Bert Perry or Art Cass, came by, cutting fallen trees off the line and repairing it. They brought us mail and news of the outside world, including the unhappy but stirring events of World War I. Other than that, our isolation was almost complete.

4

The Carefree Days of Girlhood

Our life as a family on Tomato Creek after the closing of the Halfway House was far less lonely than might be expected.

For one thing, pioneers learned quickly to be self-sufficient. For another, I guess we were too busy to miss the contacts with travelers or neighbors. Our herd of cattle now numbered more than fifty, we had a dozen horses and a growing flock of chickens. The annual job of putting up hay was a big one, and in winter the animals had to be kept in barns, in stalls well bedded with wild slough grass. In summer they pastured in pea vine and vetch that grew belly-deep on the ridges.

Luckily, the supply of hay was close to unlimited. Along Beaver Creek, three miles east of home, there were parklike open meadows and gently rolling hills grown lush with grass and vetch. Harvesting hay there was a simple task. There was almost no clearing to do, except for cutting an occasional clump of brush and getting rid of a windfall now and then.

Menzo, Elmer, and Lea all took homesteads on Beaver Creek, mostly for the hay, and built cabins for themselves. The soil was black and fertile, ready for the plow, but they never found time to do much farming.

Some of the best memories I have of those girlhood years are of climbing on one of our horses bareback and riding to Beaver Creek just for the pleasure of enjoying the beauty of the countryside.

We had one gentle old mare named Queenie that could be caught anywhere in the pasture and could be ridden with only her bell rope to guide her. I used Queenie a great deal to get the cows out of wet swampy places, where the muck was cold on my bare feet, when I went to drive them to the barn for milking at night. I also used her a lot for pleasure rides.

We had one Red Poll bull that we tried to ride, but we were never successful. One time he'd let us mount and walk off with us as docile as a plow horse. The next time he'd buck us off his back as quick as a wink.

I had a lot of fun teaching our colts and calves to lead, too. Once one of them had mastered that, I'd hitch it to a sled and lead it a quarter mile up the road. There I'd turn it around facing the barn, and slide very quitely onto the sled. Usually I had a fast, rough ride back, with snow clods pelting me in the face. But gradually I broke the young animals, especially the colts, to harness.

I never let my brothers know what I was up to, for colt breaking was considered a risky business, not fit for a girl of fifteen or sixteen. When they hitched one of the colts to a sleigh or wagon for the first time, teamed with an older and gentle horse, they often marveled that the colt took to the harness so willingly.

By practicing in secret that same way, always when Father and the boys were away for the day, I learned to ride and ride well, too. I'd lead a two-year-old colt up the road until I found a suitable stump to stand on. Then I'd slide gently onto its back and ride it home.

For the most part the colts were pets and they and I were on very good terms. Maybe for that reason, they rarely bucked, even at the outset. I was thrown only once, when other horses running up behind us spooked a young filly. I was riding bareback, with only a rope around her neck, and could do nothing to control her. She stumbled on a steep bank and fell, pitching me over her head and almost stepping on my chest when she regained her feet. She lit out for the barn, and I had a two-mile walk. Or perhaps I should say a two-mile run. I was so strong and high-spirited that I rarely walked anywhere. I still remember the feel of the cold wind in my face that day, and my long auburn hair streaming out behind me.

My love of riding finally got me into trouble. We had a beautiful coal-black stallion named Colonel, a high-stepping, stylish animal, spirited yet gentle; Father considered him too much horse for a mere girl to handle, and I was forbidden to ride him.

I felt sorry for him because he had to be kept tied in his stall or confined in a small corral back of the barn. If we let him run with other horses, he inevitably picked a fight with the geldings, and gentle-natured as he was, he fought wickedly. So, when everyone was away, hunting or making hay, I took to saddling Colonel and going for long secret rides. His high spirits matched my own, and I think one of us enjoyed those jaunts as much as the other.

My favorite destination was a certain spot on the Athabasca where I could look far upriver to the low blue line of the Martin Mountains and see the dim outline of the Swan Hills at Lesser Slave Lake.

One fine summer day, when all the men were away putting up hay, I heard the hoarse blast of the steamboat three miles away on the river. That meant they were leaving something for us at the Halfway House. Colonel needed a good run, so I decided to go and see what it was. It would be good for both of us to let off a bit of steam.

I threw a saddle on the stallion, leaped into it, and gave him his head. That was one of the most splendid rides I can recall. The horse sailed through the fields, up and over ridges, and across mudholes as if he had wings.

I have wondered many times since how Colonel would have made out as a racehorse if he had been given the proper training. He was extremely fast and as tireless as any animal I have ever known, and he loved to be let out at top speed. I have always thought that there was some close and almost human understanding between him and me. In all the times I rode him, he never misbehaved. It was almost as if he liked me too much to betray the trust I put in him.

We pulled up at the river that morning just as the stern-wheeler was nosing out from the landing. And to my chargin, the boys were there ahead of me.

They stared at me for a minute, and then gave me as severe a lecture as I ever had from any of them. I was shaking with fear. Not because of riding the stallion but because I knew that direct disobedience of my father's orders would earn me a cruel whipping if he found out about it, even though I was a girl of fifteen.

I had seen Rollo and the other boys take whippings of that kind, and I had had my own share of them. They were something to dread. I remember one time when Dad flew into a mindless rage at Rollo for no real reason, grabbed up a stick of stovewood, and beat the boy until I thought he would be killed. I watched in helpless terror, afraid to show myself lest I share in that dreadful punishment. When poor Rollo finally stumbled out of the house we ran for the barn together and kept out of our father's sight, cringing with fear, until our older brothers came home. They were big enough now to stand up to Dad and would protect us from such senseless and undeserved punishment. That unbridled temper kept me from ever feeling any real closeness to my father, and to this day it casts a black cloud over the memories of my girlhood.

I wrung from the boys that day a promise not to tell Father that I had ridden Colonel, and they kept their word. But that was the last time I ever put a saddle on the stallion. The risk of Dad's wrath was too great. The poor horse got no exercise after that, and soon became stiff in his front quarters and close to worthless. When he was six years old, Lea sold him to a traveler for one hundred dollars, a fraction of what a stallion of his kind was worth. Lea saw him a year later, and with proper exercise and care he was as spry as a colt once more.

In 1917 Dad went back to Wisconsin to marry an old school chum, Maggie Miller. He was gone for two months, and the boys and I had a wonderful time.

There was plenty of work to do, taking care of the horses and cattle and the foxes we were keeping, and we did it well. But we also found time for fun, and it was a relief to have our father away. We had all learned to play violins and guitars by ear, and we put in long evenings playing and singing as a thoroughly happy family group.

Maggie Miller proved to be a good stepmother. From the day she and Father came home, our meals were better than we had ever had. She insisted on garden vegetables, bread, cookies, and cakes, and she convinced Dad of the importance of good food. She kept all of us on the jump, but she worked as hard as we did, falling readily and willingly into the role of pioneer wife and mother.

In 1918 Menzo, Elmer, and John left home to find work, and Willie and his wife moved across Tomato Creek to live on a tract of land he had homesteaded earlier.

We had so many horses and cattle by that time that Father decided to build barns at the hay meadows instead of hauling the hay to the home place. The happiest times of my girlhood were the fall days when Lea and Rollo and I were given the job of driving the livestock up to the big meadows for the winter. The weather was usually fine, and we were on our own with nobody to boss us. The boys were healthy and strong as young bulls, and I was almost a match for them, and we enjoyed every minute of those drives.

John married and brought his wife to Tomato Creek. Next, my Aunt Mary, a sister of Father's, came to live with us, and she, John and his wife, Ruby, Lea and I journeyed twenty-five miles farther north with a few head of cows and four horses.

There was an abandoned one-room log house at Moose Portage, a lovely flat valley twelve miles down the Athabasca River from Smiths Landing. Louis Daniels had once used it as a stopover place, but he had left years before, so we moved in.

It wasn't much of a house, only one room, but we curtained off separate bedrooms for ourselves and made it comfortable and pleasant.

The boys homesteaded land at Moose Portage, and Father renounced his authority over me by making Lea and John my guardians until I became of age.

Lea got a job as a telegraph lineman at Pelican, one hundred fifty miles downriver from Athabasca Landing. Those of us at Moose Portage settled into a pleasant routine. I broke colts to ride and to work in harness, and I worked in the hayfields for nearby farmers, doing a man's work and doing it well.

It was during one of those winters that I learned a lesson I have never forgotten. Lea came home on leave from his lineman's job and went hunting one morning.

"If you hear me shoot, hitch up the team, take the sleigh, and follow my tracks down to the river," he instructed us.

Ammunition had always been costly and scarce for the Goodwins, and we had been brought up not to waste it. If he shot, it would mean that he'd have meat waiting for us.

About a mile from the house he heard a racket in a thicket, so he worked in close for a look and found two mule deer bucks fighting a no-quarter battle. They were both big deer, fairly well matched for size, but one looked old and past his prime and his rack was not as good as that of the other.

The younger animal seemed to be getting the best of the fight for he was quicker on his feet. As often as they met head on, the older buck would back him into a windfall or topple him side-wise, but the young deer could maneuver faster, and he kept ramming his horns into the rump and flank and neck of the old-timer.

Lea watched them for a few minutes and then decided to lay in a supply of venison while he had the chance. He was carrying a Winchester .32 Special, and he floored the younger buck with a shot behind the shoulder. The old fellow was a bit slow taking off, and Lea levered in another shell and dropped him, too.

He walked up to that one first. There was no sign of life in the deer, so he leaned his rifle against a tree, took out his knife, and bent over to cut its throat. The buck came to life at the first prick of the knife. It brought its hind feet up into my brother's belly, caught its hoofs in his clothing, and threw him to his knees. At the same time, a blow from one horn sent the knife flying into the snow. Then the deer was back on its feet and coming head on.

Lea got to his feet again, but the deer slammed into him and drove him back against a tree. He broke off a short piece of dry limb and jabbed it at the buck's eyes, but that didn't do much good. The deer was too enraged now, too intent on killing, to be stopped that way. Its next rush knocked Lea down and banged his head against a pine stump so hard he saw stars, but as he fell, his right hand closed around a hefty chunk of the stump, big enough to serve as a club.

The deer lowered its head, and he brought the club down behind its ears. Then he grabbed an antler, swung himself back of it, held on with his left hand and clubbed the buck as hard as he could with his right. The deer was weakening, but it still had enough strength to reach forward with its hind feet and pound the man on the legs and back. One of those blows caught Lea on the neck, cut a deep gash, and came close to finishing him, too.

In the end, buck and man broke apart and staggered drunkenly around each other, sparring for an opening. The deer was first to go down. It fell dead, and Lea fell across it and passed out. That was how another brother and I found him half an hour later when we arrived on the scene with the team and sleigh. He was lying across the buck like a sack, with his head hanging down in the snow.

By the time we revived him and got him into the sleigh, his teeth were chattering. We wrapped two horse blankets around him, loaded a deer on each side to help keep him warm, and ran the horses home at a lope. Lea was so bruised and sore he couldn't walk for days, but by a miracle he escaped serious injury.

From that day to this I have never gone close to any animal I have shot without keeping my rifle on it until I was positive it was dead. My husband later taught me to walk in from the back with the gun ready, reach around and touch the animal in the eye with the muzzle. If there is a flicker of life left, it will blink. A moose or deer or bear that doesn't is really dead.

For many years now I have gone even further than that. In my early days, when ammunition was hard to get, I never felt I could afford to waste a shell that might not be needed. But for a long time I have made it a rule to play safe by putting a final shot into the head.

5

Walter Reamer

One day in the summer of 1913, when we had been at Goodwin's Halfway House a little more than a year, a sorry-looking outfit pulled in, a makeshift and tattered covered wagon pulled by two big Clydesdales, the poorest possible sort of team for that country.

The party consisted of a mother and father, three young boys not too far from my age, and a baby girl.

The father introduced himself as Harry Reamer and told Dad that the family had moved to Canada from Illinois only a short time before. He had worked briefly at the stockyards in Calgary, and now they were on the way north to look for land somewhere along the Athabasca in the vicinity of Smiths Landing.

They had journeyed up the same dreadful mud and muskeg trail we had followed in 1911, and both horses and people showed the effects. The heavy Clydesdales, totally unsuited to the hardships of that trail, were completely played out and driven almost insane by flies. The tough and wiry smaller horses we called broomtails, such as we had driven to Tomato Creek in 1911, were able to endure far more of that kind of punishment.

And the Reamer family, especially the father and mother, were not in much better shape than their team.

"You'll have to lay over," Father told the man. "You and the horses need a few days of rest to pull yourselves together."

Reamer shook his head. "Can't," he said simply. "I don't have a red cent to pay you for keeping us or the team. We've got supplies to take us to Smiths Landing if we're careful, and we have to push along."

"It's twenty-five miles to the first good stopping place at Moose Portage," Dad told him. "The shape your team is in, you won't make that, let alone Smiths Landing. We'll put you up until you're ready to move on. We'll get some hay into those horses, and you and your family eat all you want. It won't cost you a penny."

That was the code of the northern frontier then, and it was also the best side of my father coming out.

The three Reamer boys were Lester, Walter, and Harold. The little girl was Gladys. Walter, the middle son, told me that he had been born in March of 1901, four months before my birth date in July, and he and I paired off like a kid brother and sister.

The Reamers stayed four days at the Halfway House before they moved on, and I still marvel at all the childhood fun Walter and I managed to crowd into those four days.

He knew nothing about the frontier, the way of life it imposed and the self-reliance it demanded. I knew little else.

"I'm going to be a trapper and hunter when I grow up," he boasted almost the first thing. Young as I was, I realized that he had a lot to learn before he could make that ambition come true, and I took on the role of teacher.

We started by him walking with me to the creek and carrying my bucket of water back to the house. When I went after the cows the first afternoon, he went along. And while we walked we talked about trapping and raising wild foxes to sell. I told him all I knew about baits, about setting fox traps, and feeding and taking care of penned foxes. He drank in every word, and he made me feel more important than I had ever felt in my life. My family had always been disposed to sell me short because I was the youngest child and a girl to boot. Naturally I couldn't be expected to know as much as my older brothers and sisters. Now here was this new-found playmate my own age, and a boy at that, hanging onto everything I said as if I were the wisest person he had ever encountered. I loved every minute of it.

When I went to the barn the first evening to milk, Walter tagged along. He watched me perch on the short three-legged milking stool with my head tucked against the cow's soft flank; he listened to the twin streams of milk drum into the pail.

"That looks like fun," he said. "Let me try it."

I gave him my place, and he squeezed until the cow threatened to kick him off his perch, but no milk came.

"I'll show you," I offered, and in a minute or two he had caught on to the rhythmic squeeze-and-pull, squeeze-and-pull, and was doing very well for a beginner.

He and I spent just about every hour of those four days together, and all that time I was trying to teach him the things I knew, and he was helping me at whatever chore I was doing.

The second morning I caught one of our gentle old horses and showed him how to mount and ride bareback, reining and controlling the horse with only a halter rope. I loved to ride that way, and he took to it as enthusiastically as I had. Next, I taught him to saddle and tighten the cinch.

"Gee, you're a real smart girl," he told me after his first ride in a saddle. I had never had a compliment that pleased me as much.

The morning the Reamers made ready to leave the Halfway House was an unhappy one for me. I was losing the only real playmate I had had in my twelve years, and I was close to tears. I didn't let it show, but I did whisper to Walter, I suppose with the mixed shyness and archness born in every girl, "Now I'll never see you again."

"Oh, yes you will," he promised. "When I get big I'll come back."

It was no more than a childhood promise, but I never forgot it, and he meant it and kept it.

The Reamers were a hard-luck family, totally unfitted for life on the frontier, and it was not surprising that they fell on hard times in their new location in the North.

They traveled as far as Moose Portage and squatted there, building a house but not bothering to homestead legally, prove up on their land, or pay taxes. We heard from them in round-about ways the next few years, and always the news was bad. Walter was doing well with his trapline and with the foxes he penned, the reports said, but things were poor for the rest of the family.

The mother, who was later to prove as kind to me as my own mother had been, had given birth to two more little girls, unattended by any doctor, in the first case not attended at all.

She was busy with her household work when her labor began that time. Walter was splitting stovewood just outside the house, and she called to him that she was going to have the baby and asked him to go for help.

The nearest help was an Indian woman two miles away. Walter ran those two miles, and the woman hurried back with her dog team, but when she arrived Amanda Reamer was sitting up in the bed with the baby in her arms. The circumstances were only a little better when the next child arrived, a year or two later, but at least the Indian neighbor arrived in time on that occasion.

Even in that isolated country, where hardship was the accepted lot of a woman, the Reamer family was exceptional. But in all the years I knew her, I never heard the mother complain. Whenever we talked of those hard times, she'd say quietly, "I wouldn't want to go through that again," and dismiss the whole thing.

We did not see any member of the family again until sometime in 1916 or 1917, when the father came by on foot, leading a horse he had bought at Athabasca Landing. He brought us up to date on all the bad luck that had beset them in those years.

They had lost their team of Clydesdales the first winter, when they failed to put up hay and turned the horses out to paw for grass under the snow. That was something those big draft animals were not up to. Broomtails might have made it, but Reamer's beautiful team died of starvation long before spring.

He had finally put together a raft and floated down the Athabasca to the Landing to buy the horse he was now leading home.

Long afterward I learned that the other settlers around Moose Portage blamed the Reamers themselves for most of their hard luck. If they didn't know how to get along on the frontier, they could learn from their neighbors, the reasoning went. Others were doing well in that beautiful valley, and failure had to be the fault of those who failed.

My main interest in the family was the boy with whom I had shared four such happy days, who had asked me endless questions, who had looked at me with such a clear level gaze that the girl in me responded even at twelve, the boy whose eyes smiled when his mouth showed no hint of either amusement or fondness. In the face of all the stories that reached us about the self-induced misfortunes of the Reamer family, almost everything that we heard about Walter was favorable.

Louie Daniels, who then was running a stopover place at Moose Portage, came to our Halfway House once, and I heard him tell my father, "The Reamers will never do well, but that one boy, Walter, is a good hunter and trapper. He's got three silver foxes in a pen right now, and he keeps the family in moose meat the year around. Good thing, too. They'd go hungry if it wasn't for him."

I was as pleased as if I had won praise myself.

Walter Reamer was never out of my thoughts for long during those teen-age years, despite the fact that we never saw each other. His promise to come back when he was older still rang in my ears, and there were times when I had to fight down the urge to climb on a horse and ride the twenty-five miles to Moose Portage to be with him again, even for a day or two. If a twelve-year-old girl can fall lastingly in love, I know now that it had happened to me.

About a year after Harry Reamer had come by with his horse, we heard that the family left the place where they had squatted and moved away. Nobody seemed to know where they had gone, and the word left me with a dull ache inside. Now, I told myself, I'd never see Walter again. His childhood promise would never be kept.

But in the summer of 1918 Jake Gerhart came past our place from his home at Moose Portage and told us of a Dominion Day celebration that had been held at Smiths Landing on July 1, a big frontier blowout.

I didn't pay much attention until I heard him say, "Young Walter Reamer came up and rode unbroken horses. That boy isn't afraid of anything."

My heart skipped a beat, but I tried to keep the eagerness out of my voice when I asked, "Where are the Reamers living now?"

"Grosmont," Gerhart replied. "You know, that little post-office settlement about fifteen miles north of the Landing."

I well knew, and I did my best to keep my excitement from flaring openly in my face.

It wasn't long after that before it was decided that my brothers John and Lea, John's wife, Ruby, my Aunt Mary, and I were to move to Moose Portage. Someday Walter will come back there and I'll see him again, I thought.

I was seventeen now, a pretty and lively redhead, fun loving in spite of our isolation in that remote frontier country and beginning to attract the attention of men.

Boys my own age and bachelors years older came around to court me, but I had no interest in any of them, and I cold-shouldered one after another. All but one.

He was Allen Elliott, a foreman in the railroad yard at Smiths Landing, older than I and out from England only a few years. He was a natural born gentleman, hardworking and steady, and his behavior toward me was flawless. Nevertheless, I didn't love him, and he finally won his suit only because of determination and persistence.

He walked me home one evening, and on the path some distance from the house he blocked my way. "You're not going another step until you promise to marry me," he said.

He had proposed and been rejected half a dozen times by then, but now I was half amused, half frightened by his frontal attack. It was getting dark, and I knew Aunt Mary would be concerned about me. I wanted to get on home, and for no better reason than that, in the lighthearted way of a mischievous girl of seventeen, I said, "I'll marry you. Now let me go."

He kissed me, the first and only time he ever won that privilege, and I hurried on to the house, hardly aware that I made a solemn promise.

But if I took my engagement lightly, my brothers did anything but that. In their eyes I had pledged myself to a man, and they regarded engagement fully as binding as marriage itself. To them, I was Allen Elliott's girl now, bound by an unbreakable bond.

In March or April of 1919, John and Lea went to Athabasca Landing with a team and sleigh, for supplies. When they came back to Moose Portage, Walter Reamer was with them. He walked into that one-room house and looked hard and level into my eyes, and my heart started to beat very fast, and the place became a star-spangled castle. It was the first time we had seen each other since that day six years before when the twelve-year-old boy had ridden away from Goodwin's Halfway House with his family, leaving a sad little girl behind.

In those six years, the clear-eyed boy I had liked so well had grown into as handsome and appealing a man as I had ever seen. He was six feet tall now, with wide shoulders and narrow hips lean and erect, one hundred and seventy-five pounds of very masculine man. His hair was dark brown and curly, his steady eyes were blue gray, and they still had a winsome trick of smiling while the rest of his face remained grave and still.

I knew in that first instant that I had been in love with him all those six years, and, for the first time, I realized the full significance of the promise I had made Allen Elliott.

"You shouldn't have come, Walter," I blurted out, fighting back tears.

He gave me a strange quick smile. "I had to come," he said. "We'll see."

When John and Lea went to the horse barn after supper to feed and curry their team, I walked alone to the cow barn to do the milking, and Walter followed me.

He shut the door behind him, leaned against it and went straight to the point. "They tell me you're getting married," he said, almost banteringly.

"I guess I am," I agreed. "That's what John and Lea want."

"What do you want?" he demanded.

I didn't answer.

"Your brothers wanting it is not good enough for me," he went on. "Do you love the man?"

I shook my head. And then I blurted out the story of the way my promise had been extracted.

Walter didn't laugh often, but he laughed now. "That's all I wanted to hear," he said. "I don't think you'll ever marry Elliott. Know why? You're going to marry me."

There was an endearing devil-may-care side to him, and it showed now in his twinkling eyes and in every line of his face. I was trembling all the way down to my feet, and I wanted nothing so much as to go freely into his arms, but I reminded myself that I had a promise to live up to. By the code under which I had been brought up, that stood ahead of everything else. My brothers had made me believe that the pledge I had made was the same as marriage.

But when I told Walter that, he laughed it aside. "Give your Englishman back his ring," he said sharply. "You don't belong to him and you never will." Then he smiled again. "Love me?" he asked.

"With all my heart," I answered truthfully, "but I have to keep my word."

6

The Wedding

Walter stayed on at our place for three or four days, and both of us fought down the wild desire to surrender to what we felt. He touched my hand a couple of times when he took a full pail of milk from me to carry to the house, and it was like an electric shock running through my very veins. But other than that, we kept out of each other's reach.

My two brothers seemed totally unaware of the situation that was developing under their noses. That would come a little later.

At the end of those few days, Walter went to work for a neighbor named Hagerude, on a farm a mile from our place. Before he left he said again, "I want you to give back that damned ring. I don't like to see it on my girl's hand."

I cried in bed that night, frightened at what I knew I had to do. I shared the bed with Aunt Mary, and my sobbing awakened her and she asked what was troubling me.

"I love Walter Reamer," I confessed. "I guess I have ever since I was a little kid. But I'm afraid to tell John and Lea."

I have always blessed her for what she said. "Do what your heart tells you. You can't love one man and marry another."

I returned Allen Elliott's ring the next day, as gently as I knew how. I realized he was as good a man as I would ever find, but love was not there for me to give him. I was young and high-spirited, and I suppose I was headstrong as well. But I knew my own heart and its impetuous young-girl hungers, and there was only one thing in the world I wanted. That was to be the wife of Walter Reamer.

Lea lectured me as hard as anyone ever had, and John backed him. "An engagement is not something to be tossed aside as soon as a girl sees some other man," Lea fumed. "We'll never let you marry Reamer. He's no better than a bum. He'll be a trapper all his life, but he'll never be a good one. He's fiddle-footed! He'll be forever moving from one place to another, and his wife will starve. We're not going to see you throw yourself away on a man of that kind."

He ended by forbidding me to see Walter again, and he and John followed that by warning the man I loved not to come back to our place, ever.

Our cows and Hagerude's were pasturing together. I went one evening to bring ours home, and Walter was sitting on a log at the pasture fence, waiting for me.

He got up and held out his arms to me, and, for the first time, I went freely into them and we clung to each other with the sweet, fierce intensity of young lovers everywhere. He fondled my hair, and our lips met and clung as if we could never get enough of each other. Then he released me suddenly and gave me a little shove. "Go home with your cows, woman," he ordered in mock sternness.

"Elliott has warned me to stay away from you," he said before we parted.

"What did you tell him?"

"I told him that you were my girl years before he ever saw you, and that if he didn't stand down, he was going to get a faceful of knuckles."

We went on seeing each other clandestinely all that summer, with no one but Aunt Mary the wiser. She was on our side from the beginning, and I made no effort to hide my secret and my happiness from her.

Walter and I made plans as best as we could. "I suppose we'll have to wait until you're twenty-one," he said one evening. "That will be a hard wait, but it's worth it."

"How about another girl?" I teased him. "One you wouldn't have to wait for?"

He shook his head. "You get in the way," he told me, grinning. "Every time I see a pretty girl your homely face floats between us and that ends it."

He didn't even kiss me good-night that time—just turned his back and walked away, whistling a favorite tune, one that he and I had played on the violin and guitar while he was visiting at our place.

A week later there was a basket social and dance at Moose Portage, one of those old-time frontier events where each girl packed a midnight supper in a decorated basket to be auctioned to the highest bidder. The man who bought her basket was her partner for supper, and many a romance budded and blossomed at those socials.

The rules called for strict secrecy as to the identity of the owners of the baskets. Not until the sale was made and the high bidder opened his purchase was he supposed to have the slightest inkling who his partner would be.

But I cheated. I leaked the description of my basket to Mrs. Hagerude, and she passed it along to Walter.

He led off with a high bid and kept it up. Maybe for that reason Allen Elliott, who was also at the party, concluded whose basket was being auctioned, and the bidding became a duel between the two of them. In the end, maybe because he was more reckless as well as more determined, Walter won out. He bid eleven dollars, a fantastic sum for such a privilege, and the auctioneer struck the basket, and me with it, down to him.

It was by far the highest bid made that night, and my delight at being paired openly with the man I loved was almost matched by a girl's normal pride at being queen of the social. I scolded Walter for his extravagance, but it wasn't a very convincing scolding.

"It's worth it just to sit beside you," he retorted. "On top of that, now that you're rid of the Englishman's ring I want the world to know whose girl you are."

The dancing lasted until daylight, when the farmers had to go home to take care of the morning milking, and I danced all but two or three dances with Walter. I had never known a night of such delirious happiness.

Strangely enough, Lea and John didn't scold me much when we got home, either. I suspect they knew by that time that they were fighting a losing battle and had resigned themselves to something they had no chance of preventing.

Lea left soon after that for a job on the telegraph line. John and his wife, Ruby, and Aunt Mary moved into another place about two miles away, and I divided my time between their home and the old Daniels cabin, where we had first settled when we went to Moose Portage. And, of course, I went on seeing Walter as often as I could.

Early in the summer of 1920 I rode to the Daniels place one morning to find him nailing together a flimsy raft of boards and logs, making ready to float sixty miles down the Athabasca to the Landing. At my astonishment, he held up a hand swollen and dark, with angry streaks of red running like discolored spokes up his wrist and arm.

"Blood poisoning," he explained. "I got a blister driving fenceposts, and then this happened. The quickest way to get to a doctor is by a raft."

My heart sank. "You'll never make it with one hand," I cried. "I'm going along."

He managed a grin. "No room on the raft," he told me.

"But Walter, I want to go with you," I pleaded.

He read my mind. "It's better we wait," he said quietly.

I knew he was right. If I went downriver to the Landing with him and the hand recovered, we'd be married, and running away in that fashion was counter to all my upbringing and all I had been taught to believe. But when I watched that frail raft drift away from shore into the powerful current of the river, I cried as I had rarely cried in my life. It was carrying all that was precious to me in the world, and I knew the odds were good that I might never see Walter Reamer alive again. The Athabasca was wide and swift. Would the frail raft live through ten hours of its wild buffeting?

But in a few days a letter came to Dick Mains, a bachelor neighbor who was a good friend of Walter's and happy to act as our go-between. The letter was from Walter and it was for me. He had not dared to risk sending it direct, lest someone in my family intercept and destroy it.

The hand was about well, he said, and he was staying with his father and mother a few miles out of town. He'd come back to me as soon as he could.

That September my brothers dreamed up a last-resort device to prevent my marriage. They decided to send me downriver to Pelican, to keep house for my brother Rollo. That would put me beyond Walter's reach and in a few months I'd forget him, they reasoned. Then Allen Elliott could renew his suit.

I offered no objection, but in secret I made plans of my own.

I went downriver as far as Athabasca Landing with a passing stranger in his motorboat. I was to stay with friends, the Bert

Perry family, until I could hitch a ride the rest of the way to Pelican, where Rollo was waiting for me.

I phoned Walter the minute I reached the Landing, and he was in town in an hour. Next I persuaded Bert Perry to wire my brother Lea that I was not going to Pelican at all. Walter Reamer and I had decided to be married, and he might as well give in and bless us with his consent.

We had a bit of argument by telegram, but in the end he came through handsomely, doing exactly as I asked him to. He came to the Landing in October, and on the nineteenth of that month, in 1920, I got my way at last.

Walter and I had a nice wedding. We were married in the home of a minister at the Landing, with a bridesmaid and bridegroom, a host of Walter's friends, and a dinner and dance afterward.

I still think I was a pretty bride. At least all eyes were on me. But I suppose it's only fair to assume that some were wondering what sort of wife the little frontier girl would make the handsome young Reamer.

"Where did you find her?" one of Walter's friends asked him in a bantering tone.

He pulled me close and grinned. "Oh, she was sent down to me from heaven," he said.

I didn't believe him, for in my own mind I was closer to heaven right then than I had ever been in my life.

Though my mother had named me Olive Alta, I liked my middle name best and had always been called Alta Goodwin. But when I said "I do" in response to the minister's final question of the marriage ritual that day, I was ready to make a total change and begin a completely new life. From then on I'd be Olive Reamer.

I awoke in the early daylight the next morning, and for a confused minute I thought I was still back at Moose Portage with Aunt Mary. Then I felt Walter's arm under my shoulder, and as I came wider awake I could hear the strong and steady beating of his heart. I had all I'd ever want in the world, I told myself, and I thanked God in a silent prayer for making it happen.

There was nothing then to warn me of the privation and dangers into which Walter would lead me, nothing to hint at the hardships and suffering that were to come. But to this day I cannot truthfully say I was ever sorry for one minute that I married him. I was terribly in love, and he was the one I wanted. To be nineteen years old, with life stretching ahead in shining promise, and to be the wife of your heart's desire, is worth whatever price it may exact later on. I thought that the first morning after my bridal night, and I still believe it today, more than fifty years later, when I am an old woman looking back across those years.

7

Trapper's Wife

When Walter Reamer and I struck out on our own that fall of 1920, our first home was a primitive ten-by-ten trapper's shack in Alberta thirty miles north of Athabasca Landing. We moved there right after we were married.

It was a wild and lonely place, but it was also good fur country, with fox, lynx, and bear. There were no beaver there then. They had been trapped out years before, and not until the 1940s did the game authorities reintroduce them.

The area also had plenty of game. Walter put out a trapline, and killed enough deer and moose for food. We lived on meat and bannock, which I baked on a little rusty camp stove.

I accompanied Walter everywhere he went. We had a dog team of sorts, two scrubs that weren't worth much but could pull a load of traps and other gear on a homemade toboggan. The country was beautiful, the traplines kept us busy, and I had never been happier. I was a frontier trapper's wife and that was exactly what I wanted to be. I was the daughter of a trapper and homesteader, and the isolation and hardship were nothing new to me.

We stayed in the tiny trapper's cabin only until Christmas.

Then my young husband grew restless and decided to go to Bon Accord, where he knew farmers we could work for.

The fact was, Walter was afflicted with a fatal wanderlust. For him there was always some other place where game and fur were more plentiful, opportunities better. I loved him very much, but I have to admit he had itchy feet, much as John and Lea had warned me. That restlessness was to account for much moving around in the brief years of our marriage, and in the end it led him indirectly to his death.

In the sixteen months after we were married and before our first baby, Olive, was born in an Edmonton hospital in February of 1922, we moved four times: north to a trapline, to the big farm at Bon Accord, to a coal-mining job, and then to another farm. At the two farms, Walter made twenty dollars a month, doing chores and cutting wood and fence rails, and I helped in the house for our room and board. While he worked in the coal mine I stayed with a widow a few miles away, earning my own keep, and seeing him only on Saturdays and Sundays.

I had a bad time when the baby was born. I was in the hospital three days before and fourteen days after, and we stayed on with an elderly couple in Edmonton another two weeks so I could be near a doctor. Then Walter met a man in town who was ready to go back down to Fort McMurray, on the Clearwater at its confluence with the Athabasca, where the man had worked previously and been paid four dollars a day. He said Walter could get a job there, and four dollars a day meant a small fortune in that country at that time. So as soon as I was strong enough, when our little daughter was a month old, we headed back to the raw frontier.

We got on a train on the Great Waterways Railroad, that ran from Edmonton to the end of steel at the tiny settlement of Waterways, on the Clearwater four miles above Fort McMurray. We would make that last short leg of the journey by horses and sleigh on the river ice.

What a train trip that was! We crawled along, terribly slow, and where the tracks crossed big stretches of muskeg, we could look out the window and see the mucky ground tremble and shake like open water. At one place a boxcar had been derailed, and only about two feet of it showed above the slimy ooze. I shivered at the sight of it, and I still shiver fifty years afterward, remembering it.

At Fort McMurray we moved in with my brother Frank, in two rooms above his dance hall. The place was jumping, but it was a welcome change for a young wife after her years in the bush. There were women for neighbors, children, good lively music on dance nights, people coming and going beneath the kitchen window.

Walter's first job there was driving a team of five dogs downriver to Fort MacKay, taking along the businessman who owned the dogs. That was a team to make you look twice. All but one were pure-bred timber wolves, big gray brutes that were forever backing up to get slack in their chains so that if somebody walked close enough, they could spring forward and grab him. The one that wasn't a wolf was a big red dog named Smiler. He'd curl up his lip and wag his tail when anyone approached him and he seemed extra pleased when he was being harnessed for a trip. Not so the wolves. Or if they were, they never showed it. But once in harness they were hard workers and tired far less easily than dogs.

Sled wolves were in common use there in the North at that time, and most of them were hard characters. The owners got them by digging them out of dens as pups, and they never completely lost their wolf ways. I saw a small cocker spaniel come out from behind a lumber pile near Frank's team one day. The two nearest wolves backed up until their chains were slack, and when the cocker trotted within reach they lunged and killed him before he could yelp. He was torn in two and swallowed in just a few gulps. After that I didn't wonder that Frank had warned me that if he was away and I was feeding his team, I was to throw the food to them from a safe distance and never get close.

He brought his lead wolf, Dan, upstairs to our rooms on a chain one day to give me a real close look. The animal stood as high as my chest and weighed more than I did, but Frank assured me he was as gentle as a kitten so long as his boss had hold of the chain.

I had baked bread that day and put two loaves in a box under the table to cool. The wolf smelled it, and almost before we knew what was happening he skidded Frank across the floor and went after the bread. Frank pulled and kicked and yelled, but Dan didn't raise his head until he had gulped down both loaves. Used to being fed only once a day, and forever hungry, those sled wolves were expert pilferers and could put away extra food in a hurry if they got the chance.

Their regular rations included a pound of tallow, made especially for dog teams by the Hudson's Bay Company, at each daily feeding. The driver cooked the tallow with flour and water or cornmeal mush or bannock and gave each wolf or dog three or four pounds of the mixture. If meat was available they got it instead, but that was not usually the case, at least around the settlements.

Feeding time was in the evening, for the reason that a team did not pull well on full stomachs, and a morning feeding meant a poor day's work.

Walter got back from his downriver trip in the nick of time. There were wide streams of water running between the solid ice in midriver and the shore by the time he returned, and Frank had to go out in a small boat and bring him and the dogs to the bank. I had worried for two or three days that the ice would start moving. I knew if it did and he was out on it, he'd certainly drown.

He got home on a Friday afternoon. On Sunday the two of us went for a walk on a trail that followed the Athabasca as far as Horse Creek, with Walter carrying the baby. All of a sudden we heard a thunderous noise upriver, and looking that way we could see a pile of ice like a small mountain springing up in midstream.

I had lived along the Athabasca long enough to know what that meant. The river ice had started to move and a jam was forming in the rapids a half mile above. I knew the awesome power of that ice, and knew that we needed to get back to Fort McMurray without losing a second. We were in no actual danger, for if the ice cut us off on the trail, we could climb the tar-sand hills back from the river. But those hills were brushy and rough and that would mean a very hard hike, especially with the baby. Walter wasn't as concerned as I was, for he had never lived close to a big north-country river, but he took my word for it, and we started to hurry back.

We had not gone a quarter mile when the jam began moving slowly down, and with blasts like the crash of cannon the three-foot-thick ice ahead of it, where we were, started to break and go. The Athabasca was over a half mile wide there, but there was not room in the channel for that huge, moving mountain of ice. The whole groaning, cracking mass ground and shoved its way along with unbelievable force, tearing trees out by the roots, gouging away tons of riverbank, and where the shore was low, pushing up onto the land, flattening brush and tipping trees in a smashed, tangled rubble.

At a small canyon we found it thrusting onto the shore for four hundred yards, and we made a long rough detour up the hill, and then clawed our way through thick stuff back to the trail.

Back at Fort McMurray we met a sight that was hard to believe. A huge ridge of ice was piling up on a three-acre island in the middle of the river, plowing and churning trees, earth, and rock until the whole island was ground away. Then the ice stopped moving, except for a muddy channel one hundred feet wide on our side. Another jam had formed. That jam backed the ice a mile up the Clearwater, tearing boats apart, knocking down houses, and wrecking a sawmill. Many people took refuge on the hill behind the settlement. But within an hour the pent-up force of the mighty river broke the jam, and the ice moved once more. The great piles that were left on the banks soon melted in the warmth of the spring sun, and the whole thing was forgotten.

A big stern-wheeler steamboat, the *Slavie*, was being built near the sawmill and was nearly ready for launching now. Walter got a job there toting planks. Hard work but good pay, and I was busy and happy, cooking, keeping house, and taking care of the baby.

But at the end of six days my restless young husband quit the job and almost broke my heart when he came home and announced that he had signed up with a road-building gang to work on a portage road that was being built around fourteen miles of rapids on the Slave River, between Fort Fitzgerald and Fort Smith. That meant going another two hundred and fifty miles down north, close to four hundred by river, the way we would travel, far away from the nearest doctor to a lonely outpost where I would be almost the only white woman. Frank urged me to stay behind, but Walter wanted me to go with him, and I had always believed that a wife belonged where her husband was.

We would make the long trip down the Athabasca and across the lake of the same name aboard a scow, one of two pushed ahead of a big motorboat, the *Miss Norman*. Our scow would be loaded with flour and other foodstuff at one end, a team of horses and hay and oats at the other. Our bed would be a pile of hay in the center, with blankets spread over it. We couldn't know it ahead of time, of course, but we would lose one man and a sled dog before the trip was finished.

If I had been older, I probably would have refused to go, but I was only twenty-one, and I wanted very much to be with my husband.

It was May now, and ducks and geese were as plentiful as I had ever seen them anywhere. The whole country seemed alive with them, in the air and on the water. The scenery along the Athabasca was beautiful, and all told it was a pleasant trip. But it was also scary.

The river was full of driftwood and big chunks of ice, and the scow banged into them time after time. But our skipper was Joe Bird, whom I had known years before when he was captain of the *Northern Echo.* He was an experienced boatman who knew every turn and bar as he knew the back of his hand, and he kept us out of serious trouble.

A big Hudson's Bay Company steamer churning down the river ahead of us, within sight each time we rounded a bend, didn't fare so well. It also was towing two heavy scows, one lashed on either side, and in trying to dodge a big raft of logs and ice, it crowded too close to shore. The scow on the right rammed into the bank with a pile-driver blow that broke it wide open, and the four horses it carried were in the icy water in seconds. One of the crew cut the horses' ropes and wound up in the river with them, but he grabbed one by the tail and was pulled out when the horse climbed the bank.

There was no room for the horses on the second scow, so the crew went ashore and cleared a lane through the piled-up ice on the bank to let them get to the grassy slopes above the river. They'd be rounded up again after repairs were made.

Bird stopped his boat to offer help, and no one noticed when a husky belonging to Jim Wood, the boss of the road crew Walter was to work with, jumped overboard. He was a one-hundred-dollar sled dog that Jim was taking to Fort Fitzgerald to sell. His chain let him reach the water but wasn't long enough for him to swim to shore, and when the tow started on, the poor dog was dragged under the front end of a scow and drowned.

At the mouth of the river, where it empties into Lake Athabasca, the tow had to cross nineteen miles of open water to Fort Chipewyan, where the Slave River goes out. But a strong wind from the east had piled the western half of the lake full of ice. Big chunks and broken fields of it were grinding and groaning, and there was nothing to do but camp on shore and wait for the wind to change.

We waited two days and then started out as soon as the ice had cleared sufficiently, but a bitterly cold west wind drove us aground on a sandbar, where we were stuck for hours while the men worked frantically with poles, trying to free the heavy scows. Once we were afloat again we had to turn back into the Athabasca for shelter.

We waited another two days, and by that time the Hudson's Bay steamboat caught up with us. The smashed scow had been patched up, and the four horses were riding in it again. The gas-powered boat that was pushing our scow had one advantage over the big stern-wheeler. Powered with steam, the latter had to tie up at the bank every now and then to take on a load of cordwood for fuel. Captain Bird didn't.

The wind changed, and Bird decided it would raise the water high enough to see us over the sandbars. We'd race the ice floes to Chipewyan. Almost before I knew what was happening I saw the Hudson's Bay stern-wheeler out in the lake, and everybody in our outfit was scurrying to get started.

I realized later that Walter should have put the baby and me aboard the steamboat for the crossing, to wait for him at Chipewyan, but he didn't.

The wind was churning Lake Athabasca into terribly high seas, and off to the east we could see a white line of ice drifting slowly but inexorably toward us. That was no place to be, on a scow pushed by a motorboat, and I was as scared as I had ever been.

A mile offshore the rough water began to smash the two scows together. We heard boards break, and water started to seep through. We stopped and wallowed in the seas while sacks of flour were piled over the cracks to plug the leak.

Bird took the scows in tow now, one behind the other. That kept them from banging into one another, but when Walter and I looked up from the rear one as the one ahead of us climbed to the crest of a wave, it was like looking up the slope of a gray mountain. The next minute we'd be up on the crest, staring down at the other scow and the boat. The horses had a hard time keeping their footing, and they were as frightened as I was. They reared and stomped, which made things even worse.

Within minutes Walter and I were miserably seasick. And every time we rose on a sea, I could see that towering wall of ice drifting closer and closer. From water level it looked much closer than it was, and I gave up all hope of making it across the lake. I was sure the scows would swamp or be crushed beneath tons of ice, and I called myself a hundred kinds of fool for bringing the baby into such a situation. If Walter was as worried as I was, he didn't talk about it, but maybe that was because he was too busy pumping water out of the leaky scow.

Four miles off the north shore of the lake, we came into the lee of a big island that held back the great wall of ice, and none too soon. Floating cakes were closing in around us now, and the scow smacked into those floes time after time with a crack like a pistol shot.

The mouth of the Slave at Fort Chipewyan is a bad place to get into even in good weather, with bars and rocks, and the tow arrived in the dusk of a wild and hellish night. There is no real darkness in that country in late May, June, and July, just a few hours of twilight, then daybreak again. I was tucked under the blankets with the baby when the sound of shouting brought me to my feet, just in time to see a rope tangle around a man's legs on the deck of the boat and yank him into the water and ice alongside.

We didn't see him again. Either he was crushed to death or the bitterly cold water finished him almost instantly. The tow nudged its way on into the river, dodging rocks and ice, and when I looked out again we were in quiet water between high, rock-strewn banks, with the buildings of Fort Chipewyan looming clean and white on a granite cliff to the left. I don't think I've ever seen a more welcome sight. I drew a real breath for the first time since we had come out onto Lake Athabasca.

We went ashore and followed a path up to the Hudson's Bay Company store. The far North has a strange bright beauty in its few brief weeks of summer, and I had never looked at a prettier place. Green moss and lichen covered the rocks, and blue violets and low-growing pink-and-mauve wildflowers that looked like small lady's slippers turned the cliffs and the moors beyond them into vast natural rock gardens, running off as far as we could see. The whole scene, with the white buildings perched high above the river, had a quality of emptiness and loneliness, but it also made a picture I will never forget.

The men kept watch for the body of the lost crewman the rest of that night, but he was never found.

At ten the next morning our tow and the big Hudson's Bay steamboat were under way again, down the Slave. That is a mighty river. Between Chipewyan and the place where the Peace runs into it, it averages as much as two miles wide, dotted with islands and strewn with sandbars. It's a beautiful river, but the boat pilots had no use for that stretch because the bars were forever shifting. Channels that were wide and deep one year did not exist the next, and the first boat through each season put up stakes with small flags to guide those that followed.

Five miles downriver that morning the big stern-wheeler went hard aground on a sandbar. Her paddle wheels churned the water at full speed in reverse, but the boat did not budge an inch. Bird felt his way cautiously around and went on, and that same evening he tied up at Fort Fitzgerald, with fourteen miles of rapids ahead, too rough to be navigated.

The first day at Fitzgerald, Walter and I watched as odd and savage a performance as we had ever seen, sled dogs and big northern pike or jackfish competing for table scraps thrown into the river after meals on the steamboat that had worked off the bar and caught up again by then. The water was boiling with fish turning and dodging among the swimming dogs, and I expected them to grab a husky's foot or tail, but it didn't happen.

The Slave teemed with jackfish, and probably because the water was so muddy from the high water and ice, they were swarming up every clear creek in packed, hungry schools. That was the season when the Indians caught and dried their summer's supply of fish, for themselves and their dogs.

We moved into a tent two miles north of the Fort, and when an improvident Indian offered Walter two half-starved dogs for twenty-five dollars (good sled dogs were selling for sixty to one hundred dollars apiece), he snapped them up, much to my delight. I knew that meant he was looking ahead to a winter of trapping after the road job ended. By then I had had all the moving I wanted.

We moved once more that summer, however, into a small cabin close to where the road crew was working, about halfway to Fort Smith, which is located at the lower end of the rapids that begin at Fitzgerald. Walter and the other men put that cabin up in one Sunday. It was only ten by twelve, with the bark still on the logs, a pole-and-sod roof, and a dirt floor with roots and stubs sticking up. But it would do, for we'd be living in it only through July and part of August, and I was completely happy once more.

We were less than half a mile from one of the wildest rapids on the Slave, and the roar of the water was like low thunder day and night. A few times on Sundays we pulled fly nets over our heads, covered the baby with a specially made net, and walked down to the river to watch it pound driftwood and logs to pieces against huge rocks.

Looking back, I suppose that was as good a summer as I had ever had. Now that the dangers of our long trip north from Fort McMurray was past, I realized that we had had a ringside seat for one of the great spectacles of the North, the annual breakup of the ice, the age-old prelude to the arctic spring. It had been a majestic thing to see, but it had also been terrifying, and I had no wish ever to witness it again.

What I wanted now was to get back to Fort McMurray and enjoy a winter of such comforts as that lonely little outpost afforded.

8

Trapline Winter

The scow was heavy and cumbersome, an old thirty-footer that Walter and I had bought at Fort Fitzgerald. But we didn't have much plunder, and with only two grown-ups, a baby, and a pair of sled dogs on board, it rode high. The deep steady current of the Slave pushed us north far faster than a man could have walked on shore.

The scow had oars and now and then Walter grew impatient and used them for a short distance, but there was no need for it. Mostly he just steered enough to hold to the middle of the channel, and we watched the early-fall scenery slip past along the banks or played with our six-month-old daughter, Olive. When we weren't cuddling her, she slept as contented as a kitten in the small cardboard box that served for her bed.

Muskrat sign was plentiful along the river, and there was lots of old beaver work, lodges, and the evidence of dams, but nothing recent. The beaver had been trapped out of that country then, but have since made a comeback and are abundant again now. We saw deer and moose tracks on the sandbars, and flocks of ptarmigan fed in the willows on the river bottoms. Wherever there was green grass along the shore, snow geese pastured by the hundreds. We were rarely out of hearing of their wild voices, either by day or during the half-light of the short arctic night.

Where the Salt River came into the Slave we went ashore at a camp where Indians were drying fish. A cluster of smoke-blackened tents stood on the bank; men, women, and children were all over the place; and gaunt sled dogs were tethered to stakes, their wild and eerie howling echoing across the river. Fish by the hundreds, split open, were drying on pole racks. Mostly jackfish or northern pike, and goldeyes, with a few big "coney fish" mixed in. They were inconnu, known as the sheefish in many places in the Arctic, weighing an average of eight to twelve pounds.

When we left the camp the Indians gave us enough fish for our evening meal, for ourselves and our two dogs. We had come to a land of plenty, we agreed, a dream country for a young trapper and his family. Fortunately we had no inkling of what lay ahead.

The time was late August. The trip had come about when Walter met two trappers, Nels Nelson and Pete Anderson, at Fort Fitzgerald. The road job he had worked on through the short summer was finished about the middle of August, and then along came Pete and Nels.

They had trapped the fall before down the Slave at Grand Detour in Northwest Territories, one hundred miles upriver from Great Slave Lake, they told him. They had come out before Christmas, they said, with sixteen hundred muskrat skins that brought a dollar fifty apiece. There were lakes all over the country between the Slave and the Little Buffalo, they told Walter, and every one of those lakes crawled with marsh rats.

My husband was a rover, and above everything else he was also a trapper at heart. For him, stories of that kind were like wild tales of a gold strike. He gave up then and there all thought of our plans to go back to Fort McMurray, on the Athabasca River two hundred fifty miles south, where I had been looking forward to the presence of other white women, a few frontier comforts, and a doctor in case I or the baby needed one. The three of us, Walter decided, would spend the winter trapping on those rich fur grounds.

So we bought the scow and thirty-four single-spring traps, a pair of three-foot snowshoes, and enough babiche (rawhide) to make a larger pair. The small ones were for me. Walter would fashion his own before snow came. We also bought four hundred pounds of flour, fifty pounds of white sugar, and four fifty-pound sacks of potatoes. I remember that we paid twelve dollars for each of those sacks. Coal oil was two dollars a gallon at Fitzgerald. We added beans, rice, salt pork, oatmeal and baking powder, salt, tea, and cornmeal for the dogs, and our grub list was complete.

The scow was hauled across the fourteen-mile portage between Fort Fitzgerald and Fort Smith, over the road that Walter had helped to build, and the Mounties at Fort Smith checked our supplies to make sure they were adequate. That was a standard procedure then with anyone going into Northwest Territories for the winter. It was a sensible requirement, too, for the winters there are long and cold, and the hardships can be terribly severe.

We loaded the scow and shoved off on August 23, 1922, on the long slow trip down the Slave to our trapping grounds. We were in completely unfamiliar country, for it was the first time either of us had been that far north. So far as we knew there'd be no whites within fifty miles of where we were going. We had no idea where or what our winter home would be. But we were on the way into what Walter had been told was good fur country, and he was completely happy. I didn't face quite as cheerfully as he did the prospect of wintering with a child not yet a year old, hundreds of miles from the nearest doctor.

Nels and Pete had said to look for an old sawdust pile where a sawmill had once stood, on the west shore of the river, and settle down around there some place. We passed the sawdust pile on the fourth day of floating. Nels had also described another landmark, a high cut-bank some distance below the old mill site, with a tumbledown cabin perched on the very edge of the bank where the shore had caved away in times of high water.

We found the cabin exactly as he had described it, half rotted away, forlorn and lonely looking. Just below the high bank, whoever had lived there at one time had made themselves a good boat landing, and it was just what we were looking for. We tied up the scow, let the two dogs loose for a run, got the tent up, and carried our supplies and outfit up the bank. It was close to midnight when we finished. We tied the dogs to trees and turned in.

We were no more than asleep when I was awakened by some animal gnawing on the slab of salt pork that we had brought into the tent for safekeeping. At first I thought one of the dogs had gotten loose, but as my eyes grew used to the dim light in the tent I made out a large skunk instead.

The tent was only a nine by twelve, and the skunk was working on the pork within three feet of my face. I shook Walter awake, and we tried to drive the animal off, but he wouldn't budge.

"I'll have to shoot him or we won't have any pork left," Walter said finally. We knew that wasn't a very good idea, but we had little choice.

I can report that shooting a skunk inside a tent is a big mistake. Whoever invented tear gas simply copied an idea that skunks have used for thousands of years.

Walter's rifle cracked. It wouldn't be truthful to say the air turned blue, for it was too dusky in the tent to distinguish colors. But it certainly turned something. Our eyes started to water, we were half blinded, and began to gag. I grabbed up the baby and fumbled my way outside. After a minute or so Walter stumbled out behind me, dragging the dead skunk. He threw it over the riverbank, and we hauled our bedding outside, spread it under a big spruce, and spent the rest of the night in the open. Luckily we were tired enough to sleep anywhere.

The next morning we moved the tent a few hundred feet down the hill and carried all our belongings over to it. But it was many days before the overpowering smell of skunk subsided, and I told my husband more than once, somewhat reproachfully, that his way of saving the slab of salt pork was worse than useless. The pork smelled almost as bad as the tent.

Next we started work on a log cabin, twelve by sixteen, for a winter home. Walter cut and notched the trees, and together we carried them up to the site and rolled them into place. An Indian woman at Fort Fitzgerald had given me a small hammock for the baby. I slung it between two trees, put little Olive in it, tucked mosquito net carefully around her to keep off the millions of mosquitoes and blackflies, and the child slept and cooed and amused herself while we worked.

In two weeks the cabin was up, windows in and door hung, and a bunk bed built. I cut hay with a butcher knife for a mattress, built cupboards out of wooden packing boxes, and Walter and I settled down in the nicest house of our own that we had had since we were married.

There was one drawback. We had left the bark on the logs, and as soon as our stove warmed the place, big black spruce beetles came out from under that bark. They bit savagely, and I was more afraid of them than I would have been of a bear. After all, I had been used to bears all my life, but not to beetles.

It was still too early to start trapping, so Walter took trips each day to scout the country, look for game and fur sign, and locate the lakes where the muskrats were. It took only a few of these trips for him to realize that we had picked the wrong place for winter headquarters. He found little sign of fox, lynx, or coyote, and the nearest lake on our side of the river was ten miles away. This was not the place that had been described by the two trappers back at Fitzgerald, and my husband was plainly worried. He'd sit in the evenings, thinking hard, and wouldn't even hear me when I spoke to him.

We had built a tiny, cranky canoe, nine feet long, using willow trunks hewed flat on one side for the ribs and frame. Walter sawed the planks, a quarter inch thick, out of a birch log with a crosscut saw. They were only six or eight inches wide, and it took a lot of them to complete the job. The planking was covered with canvas, four coats of paint were put on, and we had a serviceable one-man canoe. After one trip in it, with Walter and the baby, I decided firmly that it was not a family craft. From then on, I promised myself, I would stay ashore until we got a better boat.

We made that one trip, down the Slave, to look for muskrat country. Four miles below our cabin we found a lovely clear creek running in, and stopped to catch jackfish. We tried fishing from the canoe, but it was too unsafe, so we got out on the sandy shore and started to fish from the beach.

I decided to use two lines. I stuck one pole in the ground and picked up the second, and when I turned around I had a nine-pound pike on the first one. I dropped the other outfit but had no more than started to haul my catch in when the second pole started to slide toward the water. I had a seven-pounder on that line. I yelled for help, and before Walter could get my second fish in he was fast to a four-pounder of his own. We fished with one line apiece after that. I caught eighteen big jackfish about as fast as I could take them off the hook, and Walter did as well. When we loaded the catch into the canoe and started back upriver, the gunwales were hardly more than an inch above the water. I resolved not to go out in that craft again.

I made jackfish booyah, a favorite dish of ours, for supper that night. Booyah is a common term all through the north country for soup or stew. Probably the name comes from the French bouillon, or maybe from bouillabaisse, the famous fish soup of France. To make it with jackfish, you scale and clean the fish, strip the skin off in one piece like a sock, and lay it aside for later use. Boil the whole fish in salt water for ten or fifteen minutes, until the meat flakes off the bones easily. Mix the meat, fresh mashed potatoes, and dry bread crumbs and stuff it all into the uncooked skin. Tie the ends, put it back in the salt water, and cook until it is thoroughly heated through.

Shortly after we got back to our cabin that afternoon, a muskrat clambered up the riverbank and waddled slowly toward our dogs. The nearest dog, Snap, backed away to get slack in his chain, and the rat misunderstood the action for retreat. It bared its teeth and made a run for the dog. Snap lunged, killed the rat with one shake, and tore it apart and swallowed it in a few gulps. It was the best meal he had had in quite a while. He licked his chops, lay down, and tucked his nose into his tail as if nothing had happened. I can still hear the other dog, Dan, whining softly in envy as the rat went down.

The next morning I suggested to Walter that he scout for lakes on the opposite side of the river. Perhaps we had misunderstood Nels Nelson's directions. The Slave was a mile wide, and my heart was in my throat while I watched my husband paddle across in that miserable little canoe. But he came back in late afternoon and said there was no end to the marshy country he had found, dotted with small lakes, with muskrat houses on all of them.

We knew then that we had built our cabin on the wrong side of the river. It would be dangerous to cross as long as the water was open, and once the Slave started to freeze over, and while it was breaking up in the spring, Walter could not get across at all. Those were the best times to trap. Heartsick as I was at the idea of leaving the place we had fixed up so nicely, there was no choice.

We had torn the scow apart to make doors and windows. That left only the canoe, and it was not adequate for the move to the other shore, so I suggested to Walter that he build a boat. After he was marooned across the river by a windstorm and had to stay overnight without food or bedding, he agreed.

It was a clumsy boat, without much taper at the bow, for we had no way to bend the heavy boards of the scow, but it was far better than the canoe. We moved to the west side of the Slave and started another cabin. Planning to live in it only until November, when the lakes froze and we'd have to quit trapping, we threw it up hurriedly, of small green logs, using the door and windows from our first place. It was soon finished, and about October 1 we put our traps out.

Circumstances altered our plans, and we stayed on in that rough little cabin until spring. For one thing, there was far more fur on the west side of the river, mink as well as muskrats. There was also more firewood handy, and the cabin stood in a thick grove of spruce, where it was sheltered from the wind.

For those reasons, and also to save ourselves another move and the work of repairing the first cabin and putting back the door and windows we had removed, we did not go back to the place on the east side of the river in November.

That proved a disastrous mistake. We had left our fishhooks, lines, and net at the original location. Before spring the lack of that gear was to play a major role in bringing us to the brink of starvation. Too, if we had moved back to the east bank for the winter months, we would have been in contact with the dog teams that were hauling mail on the ice of the Slave once a month. The drivers of those teams could have helped us, and we would have been spared the most terrible ordeal I have ever known.

As it was, there was no occasion for us to make a trail from our new cabin to the river. We did not see a living soul until winter was well along, and no one outside knew where we were. I realize now that it was a foolhardy piece of business, and it brought the three of us very close to death.

At least the trapping prospects looked good. But now we faced another problem. Wild meat was scarce enough to cause us worry. There was not a moose or deer track anywhere. Caribou came through now and then, crossing from one range of hills to another, and wolves followed them, but the caribou could not be relied on for a meat supply.

It was at least sixty miles from the Little Buffalo River to the moss-covered hills east of the Slave, and before winter closed in we had named that belt of scrub timber and swampy lakes Starvation Wilderness. Snow came to stay on October 10, and after that the whole country lay white and lifeless, without even the chickadees and Canada jays that we had expected to see in the winter woods.

Trapping was good. We were looking at the traps twice a day and coming back to camp with as many as a dozen muskrats. We would hike out to the lakes together, then I would take the baby and the dog team with a small toboggan and cover half the line. Walter would go over the other half with a packsack, skinning his rats as he took them from the traps. We'd meet at midday, and on the way back to camp he would cover my end of the line, I would take his. That afforded a change of scenery and also gave the rats time to fill the traps again.

We trapped until the first of November, when the lakes froze and the temperature dropped too low for us to be out in the wind and cold. From December until the end of March it rarely climbed as high as 10 degrees below zero, and there were days when it went to 65 below. The wind was like a knife, and we huddled in our poorly chinked shack and tried to cut enough spruce and willow to keep warm.

Spruce and balsam pitch dripped from the roof poles. I had curly auburn hair that reached to my waist, and Walter thought that was my crowning glory. But now it began to get fouled and matted with pitch. I couldn't comb it or wash it out, and gradually those long curls turned to tangled rattails.

I put up with it for a month. Then one day when Walter was off looking at fox traps I took scissors and cropped it as close to my head as I could.

The barbering left me a funny-looking sight. When my husband walked into the cabin he took one look; I saw his face go gray, and then, without saying anything, he turned his back. Finally he asked, "Where is the hair?" I pointed to a corner near the door, where I had pitched it, intending to burn it later. He retrieved two or three curls that were free of pitch and put them in a small box. "Don't throw that out," he told me. "I want to keep it." Neither of us guessed then how few of our meager possessions would be left to us when spring came.

My hair grew back, of course, but it was never as pretty after that. Bobbed hair soon came into style, and I never let mine grow long again.

We managed through that bitter winter until February. By then we knew we would run out of food long before June, when we had planned to catch the first steamboat coming up the Slave from the Arctic. We had known since October, too, that I was pregnant again. Our second baby would be born in July. We didn't dare to wait for the boat, knowing that before the end of winter we would have nothing to eat.

One cold afternoon in early February, to our complete astonishment, there was a knock at the cabin door. When we opened it a tired-looking old man with a ragged gray beard was standing there. He was so weak he staggered as he walked in.

He told us his name was Garvin and that he had been trapping on the east side of the Slave fifteen or twenty miles downriver. He was on his way out to Fort Smith and had seen our smoke from the river. "I'm sick," he explained. "Something wrong with my gums. I get so weak I can't hunt or tend my traps."

In my whole lifetime I have never known a wilderness trapper to develop scurvy, but I still wonder if Garvin was not a victim of it.

He told us that he had made one trip to the hills east of the Slave to hunt wolves for bounty, and had shot seventeen in four days. Wolf packs were following the caribou herds there, he explained, and he had counted as many as ten caribou kills in a day. It was good hunting, but he was too ill to go back.

He stayed with us for two days. At the end of that time he felt so much better that he decided he could make it through until spring breakup. So he turned around and headed back to his trapping grounds. We never saw him again.

For some reason, the old trapper's visit seemed to crystallize our plans to leave this frozen wilderness while we could. Walter and I talked things over and agreed there was nothing to be gained by waiting longer. Once the baby and I were safe at Fort Smith, he'd come back to the cabin and wait for the spring trapping when the lakes opened.

We were in no shape for the sixty-mile trip out. Our two dogs were old, half starved, and not strong enough to pull the baby and me on the sled. Little Olive could ride, but I would have to walk. Nor did we have suitable clothing for cold of 40 and 50 degrees below. But we outfitted ourselves as best we could.

I made a parka for myself out of an old blanket and covered it with canvas. Walter had only buckskin pants and moccasins, a sweater, and a wool jacket over everything. What we lacked were fur parkas and fur-lined moccasins. But as our food dwindled and no moose or caribou tracks, not even a sign of rabbits, marred the clean snow around us, we grimly made ready for the trip.

We put hot water in a water bottle, heated stones, wrapped little Olive in our whole bedroll of four blankets with the stones and water bottle beside her, and struck out up the Slave. The empty toboggan was all the dogs could pull.

It was bitterly cold, probably around 40 degrees below, the going was hard, and we made poor time. Mail was being carried up and down the Slave that winter by dog team, and the teams had packed a pretty good trail on the ice, but snow had drifted over it, and we couldn't follow it. When we left it we were plodding through two feet of soft snow. The day was sunny, and the glaring light hurt our eyes and made it hard to see where we were setting our feet.

The dogs pulled willingly enough for a while, but the heavy going was too much for them. After about fifteen miles they began to give out. They stopped frequently, and more than once they lay down in the snow. Walter urged them on and pushed all he could on the toboggan handles to help, but we both knew we weren't going to go much farther. We tried to hurry, knowing darkness was not far off, but there was not enough strength left in either me or the dogs for that.

The winter days are very short there in the North, and by three thirty in the afternoon, dusk was beginning to come down. The dogs followed the mail-team's trail across the river to the east bank—and there was a little cabin with smoke curling out of the chimney. I can't remember that I was ever gladder to see a human habitation.

The cabin belonged to two young trappers, and we pulled in thinking we would stay the night there. But there wasn't room to walk between the stove, beds, and table, and it was plain that short of a life-or-death matter the trappers couldn't put us up. We had tea and bannock, and they told us that four miles farther up the Slave, at the sawdust pile we had passed on the way down-river back in August, another trapper, Bert Bennett, had a comfortable cabin. We rested a little while and started for Bennett's place, with the early darkness thickening over the white wilderness. We had come nineteen miles so far that day, and I didn't feel as if I could travel another five hundred feet, much less four more miles.

That was a terrible hike. Each mile of the four seemed like ten. The dogs stopped every few yards to lie down in their harness, and Walter went ahead to break trail and pull them along with a short length of rope while I pushed on the toboggan handles for a change. It was too dark for him to see where he was putting his snowshoes, and he must have fallen a hundred times. Pain stabbed at my legs, back, and all through my body. I realized finally that I was leaning on the toboggan handles more than I was pushing.

It seemed that the easiest thing to do would be to walk off into the snow and lie down and sleep forever. But there was the baby to think of. I could hear her whimper now and then, and I wondered vaguely whether she was freezing. There was nothing to be done about it if she was. She wasn't hungry, for she had been fed at the trapper's cabin, and I didn't dare open the bedroll she was wrapped in to look at her.

I just kept putting one foot ahead of the other, stumbling and staggering along, exhausted and terribly cold, until I lost all track of where we were or how far we had come. That is all I recall of the last mile or two.

A shout from Walter brought me partly out of my stupor. "Hello, there!" he yelled. I looked ahead and could see a square of light shining out of a window. Oh, Lord, what a welcome sight!

Afterward I could not remember the trapper Bennett opening the door or me and the baby being carried into the warmth of the cabin. The first thing I recalled was Walter pulling off my coat and moccasins. Then somebody set a bowl of hot soup in front of me, and my husband shook me and told me to eat.

In a daze I watched Bennett take off the baby's rabbit-skin coat and start to feed her. They said afterward that I cried, "No, don't take her coat off. She'll freeze!" but I had no memory of that. I did not even realize that we were safe and warm inside four walls. The next thing I knew, gray daylight was filtering in the window of the cabin, and Walter was telling me to get up for breakfast.

I was too stiff and sore to make it, but he pulled me out of bed and made me move my legs and body. It's surprising how much power of recovery a person has at twenty-one. I was four months pregnant, had run and walked twenty-three miles the day before in deep snow—and when Bennett looked at his thermometer that morning it was 61 degrees below! The wonder was that the three of us had not frozen to death on the trail.

We knew now that we could not make it out to Fort Smith with our dogs and outfit. It would be dangerous and foolhardy to try. Luckily, Bennett had extra supplies that he could spare. He sold us flour and beans enough to see us through, and even loaned Walter twenty-four good muskrat traps.

We stayed there three days, while little Olive reveled in a big board floor to toddle around on and I regained my strength. At the end of that time the whole Reamer family was as good as new, and the dogs had been stoked with enough food that they were in better shape than when they began the terrible trip upriver. Walter and I were ready to go back to our cabin and see the winter out. With muskrats at a dollar fifty each, there was good money to be made as soon as the lakes started to open. When the first boat came up the Slave we would be waiting for it, sitting pretty. Or so we thought, at least.

Bennett advised us to go back to our cabin by a different route, not to follow the mail team's trail on the river. We could save five miles, he said, by taking a cutoff through the bush on what was called a river snigh in that country—a channel or small creek made when the Slave was in flood in early summer.

We started out on a clear morning, with the sun shining through a thin haze of frost. Wind had drifted and packed the snow solidly enough that we seldom broke through, and the going was easy. We pulled up in front of our lonely little cabin just as it was coming full dark—and not more than two hundred feet from the door was a fresh moose track cutting across the snow. Had we been home, that moose would have meant meat for the rest of the winter, and the dogs needed it even more than we did.

The forty-six-mile sled trip up the Slave to Bennett's and back had been heartbreaker enough, with death from hunger looking over our shoulders. Missing a chance at the moose was the hardest blow of all.

It has been almost fifty years since that evening when we drove our two gaunt dogs up to the door of the cabin in the winter dusk and saw the track, but I still remember that as one of the most discouraging moments of my life.

Fortunately, we could not foresee that there was worse to come.

9

Spring of Starvation

The moose tracks led off into scrubby spruce, away from the river. If Walter could kill the maker of those tracks, it would mean meat for the remaining weeks of winter, and the bones and leavings would supply urgently needed food for our dogs. Walter poked shells into my old .25/35 Winchester carbine, the best rifle we had, and took the track right after breakfast the next morning. He had a rifle of his own, a .303 Savage, but it was in bad condition, hardly safe for shooting, and he had very little ammunition for it.

He followed the moose all that day without catching sight of it, made a fire and camped under a spruce tree in below-zero cold that night, and took the trail again at daylight the next morning. But the moose was traveling through the country and kept going, and by early afternoon of the second day Walter had to give up. His homemade snowshoes were wearing out, and he was getting so far from camp that he did not dare to keep on. He got back to the cabin after dark, tired and sick with disappointment, and I felt as bad as he did. That was the only moose track we had seen, and the closest we had come to killing fresh meat through the whole winter.

We did not see or hear a living thing except each other and the dogs, and three foxes that Walter trapped, until the end of March. It seemed as if all the game, even rabbits, had left the area or died off. Neither of us had ever seen a winter wilderness as lifeless and still as that country along the Slave.

We fed the three fox carcasses to the dogs, and the poor animals were starved enough to gulp the smelly fox meat down with relish. The beans and flour that Bert Bennett had sold us were running low, and we were eating less than half of what we wanted.

In desperation, toward the first of April we decided to start mink and muskrat trapping, despite the fact that the lakes and marshes were still covered with three or four feet of iron-hard ice. It wasn't so much that we wanted fur as that we needed the muskrats desperately for food for ourselves and the dogs. None of us would last much longer without a supply of meat.

We made a trip to the nearest lake, where we had trapped before freeze-up, taking the baby on the toboggan—and found the shallow, swampy lake frozen solidly to the bottom. Not a muskrat was left alive. We went on to two or three other lakes farther away, and the situation was the same. When we turned the dogs back toward camp that afternoon we were about as disheartened and worried as two people could get.

On the way home we came across the tracks of nine timber wolves that had milled around our outbound toboggan track earlier, and when our dogs tucked their tails between their legs and started to skulk along with their bellies to the snow, we knew the wolves were following us, just out of sight. In thick willows along a creek bed we heard twigs break, and the hair on the necks of the dogs stood on end. We weren't afraid of the wolves for ourselves, at least not by daylight, but we did pity the dogs. Back at the cabin we drove them right to the door, unharnessed them, and took them inside with us.

The wolves howled around us most of the night, the dogs

cowered in abject fear, and in the morning we found the snow crisscrossed with wolf tracks in every direction. But the pack had disappeared at daylight, and that was the last we saw of them.

A few days after that, we packed up the little food we had left, our tent, bedding, and traps and went eight miles west to some bigger lakes that Walter had found while he was tracking the moose.

We put up the tent at the first lake, found water under the ice, cut into muskrat houses, and caught a few rats. That eased the pinch of hunger, but we were not taking enough for ourselves and the dogs, and at last Walter made the unhappy announcement that they would have to be destroyed. Although I realized that that was kinder than to let them starve, the idea broke my heart, and I coaxed him to wait a few more days in the hope the weather would turn warmer and trapping would pick up.

Instead, it turned bitterly cold and stayed that way for eight days. Before the end of the cold spell the dogs were so hungry they whined and howled for food almost continuously, and finally Walter shot them. It had to be done, but I cried about it until I was sick.

Less than a week after that the weather broke. The sun came out warm and bright, the snow started to melt, and the lakes opened up around the shores. We began trapping and shooting muskrats by the dozens. If the night was cold and ice formed, our luck fell off. Some days we took only five or six pelts, but one day before the fur spree was over we took seventy. Walter followed the trapline from daylight to dark, and I was kept busy every minute skinning rats and stretching the pelts, making stretchers by bending willow sticks into shape.

We were living on muskrat meat and having enough to eat for the first time that winter. I boiled it and gave our little daughter the broth, from her bottle, and she thrived on it.

When spring comes to the North it comes with a rush. The

white silence of winter is broken, suddenly it is sunny day after day, and the days are long and warm. But the short dark hours of the spring nights are often cold, and it was hard to keep warm in our tent, even with a fire in the tiny stove.

We were wet most of the time, from wading out into the icy water to retrieve rats we shot, and our clothing did not have time to dry thoroughly overnight. But we were taking a rich harvest of pelts and saw no reason to complain. After the hunger and hardships of the winter, this trapline springtime was a welcome season indeed.

We continued trapping while the snow melted, and the creeks rose and became treacherous little rivers. Walter and I agreed that we'd stay camped at this lake until May 10. Then we would hike back to the cabin, go up the Slave to Bert Bennett's place by rowboat, and there catch the first steamer of the season to Fort Smith.

But things don't always go as people plan them. On the morning of May 2 I was baking bannock in the little stovepipe oven in the tent. I stepped outside to look for Walter, saw him coming a quarter mile up the lake, took the baby by the hand, and walked to meet him. Little Olive was toddling all over now.

There were rats swimming in the open water along the shore, and I kept back far enough not to frighten them. Every now and then Walter would stop and pick off one with his Remington .22. When we met, I took part of his load of fresh pelts, and the three of us started back.

All of a sudden we heard ammunition exploding at a terrible rate, and then smoke and flames rolled up around the tent. Walter dropped his sack of fur and ran, and I grabbed our daughter and hurried after him. When I got to the tent, he was dragging out charred foodstuff and burning pieces of blankets. I grabbed the things as he pulled them out and doused them in the lake.

It was all over in ten minutes. A tent disintegrates fast in a fire.

What we had saved would have made a very small bundle. Two or three half-burned pieces of blanket, a few matches in our pockets and in a waterproof container. Walter's .22 that he had been shooting rats with was safe, and my .25/35 had been standing outside the tent. There were four shells in its magazine, and Walter had a box for the .22 in his pocket. The rest of our ammunition was gone. We also pulled a scorched .22 Stevens of mine out of the burned tent. It was damaged, but looked as if it could be fired. We didn't even have a piece of canvas big enough to wrap the baby in if rain came.

Most of our rat pelts had been hanging in a tree outside the tent and were safe. We had lost only ten or twelve that were inside drying. But one of the possessions I loved most was gone—the violin my brother Lea had given me for my sixteenth birthday. Right then that birthday seemed a long time back.

Of our food we had salvaged about four cups of flour, wet and mixed with cinders, a pound or so of beans, and a little bannock. For the baby, luckily, there were a few cans of condensed milk left undamaged.

That scanty handful of supplies would have to see us through, with muskrat meat, until we could reach Bennett's cabin. We faced a hard hike of eight or ten miles without dogs, through flooded and difficult country, and then twenty-three miles in a crude and clumsy rowboat against the spring current of the mighty Slave. Worst of all, we could not start the trip upriver until the Slave broke up, and we had no way to forecast when that would happen.

We knew that the ice went out of the Athabasca around the middle of May, but we asked each other hopelessly when the breakup was due on the Slave.

Things looked grim. I was expecting our second baby in a

little more than two months. There'd be a rough time ahead. But there was no use sitting by the ruins of the tent and worrying about it. The thing to do now was to get started.

We hung our traps in trees where they could be found the following fall, ate our bannock and a good meal of muskrat we had roasted earlier, rolled the baby in the charred patches of bedding, and lay down under a tree to rest for a few hours. We did not dare to spare matches for a fire. The few we had must be hoarded for times of genuine need.

When we awoke we made up our loads and were ready to start. I wrapped our daughter in the blanket pieces and tied her in with babiche, to be carried on my back Indian style. The little toddler was so thin she wasn't very heavy. Next I rolled one cooking pot, knives, forks, spoons, a cup, and the baby bottle in a scorched scrap of blanket and tied it all on behind. We tied the two .22s and the .25/35 together in one bundle. I would carry that like a suitcase.

Walter's load would consist of the dry muskrat pelts, about two hundred and fifty in all, our stove—it weighed only ten pounds—and three lengths of stovepipe. He had fashioned a home-made packsack, big and roomy, from a gunnysack and rope. By shoving as many rat skins down in the bottom as the sack would hold, nose down, then telescoping a second tier inside those, and continuing the process until the sack was jammed to the top, we managed to pack our total catch. A fur buyer back at Tomato Creek had showed me that trick years before.

We left the burned-out camp with me carrying all I could handle and Walter packing a load of close to one hundred and ten pounds. In the late winter we had traveled eight miles coming to that lake from our cabin. Now we must cover between sixteen and twenty going back. Every creek was roaring full and two or three times its usual width. We detoured miles to find places where we could wade across, and then had to follow the streams back to our blazed trail to avoid getting lost. Many times Walter had to make three trips through the swollen and icy creeks, one with his pack, one with the baby and my load, and a third to help me across.

It took us two days of the hardest kind of travel to get back to the cabin. At the end of the first day we stopped, made a shelterless camp under a clump of spruce, and roasted a muskrat we had brought along. Near this place we had cached several rat carcasses on a high rack of poles earlier, hanging them so they would dry, against possible future need. After supper Walter went to get them.

He came back looking very glum. A wolverine had raided the cache, and there was not a rat left. We went without breakfast and our noon meal the second day, but in the middle of that afternoon I shot a small muskrat in a slough. It wasn't big enough to make a good meal for one hungry person, let alone three, but we stopped and cooked it on the spot and divided it up.

It was midnight when we trudged wearily up to our cabin, tired, discouraged, and hungry. But at least we had a roof over our heads again, and four walls to keep out the cold at night. Going to bed supperless didn't seem too bad.

When daylight came, I got up and picked out all the dried beans I could find, where I had discarded culls during the winter. I also scraped every empty flour sack for the little flour that remained. Then I cooked the beans and baked a bannock from the flour, dirt and all.

One look at the Slave that morning confirmed our worst fears. Water was running between the ice and shore. We couldn't get out on the river and wouldn't have dared if we could. There was no hope of following the shore up to Bennett's place, either, because of the many large creeks that came in. We had no choice but to wait for the ice to go out.

10

Escape

Walter started to calk the rowboat and cover the seams with pitch. I put in the time hunting, looking for muskrats, ducks, squirrels, even small birds, anything edible. My total kill the next five days consisted of three red squirrels. It wasn't much, but it helped.

Then the worst disaster of all struck. On May 10, with ice still solid in the river, Walter and I split up to hunt. He took the baby piggyback and went in one direction, I in the other. He was carrying his Remington .22, and I had the fire-damaged Stevens that we had salvaged from the burned tent. Those were the only guns for which there was sufficient ammunition now.

I scared up a flock of mallards, but they flushed out of range. Then, at the edge of a small muskeg a half mile north of camp, I saw a rabbit hunched under a clump of brush, the first one I had seen since fall. I had never wanted game more than I wanted that rabbit. I rested the .22 against a small tree and pulled the trigger. All I remembered afterward was fire in my face, blinding light, then a numbness in my nose and eyes.

I never knew how long I leaned against that tree. I couldn't see, my ears rang, and there was terrible pain from the bridge of my nose through my right eye and clear around to my ear. Slowly the weakness went out of my legs, and I stamped the ground in agony. I couldn't get the right eye wiped dry, and the more I wiped it the worse it hurt.

At first I didn't know what had happened. Then I remembered that I had tried to shoot a rabbit. I felt around on the ground and found the gun. Next I looked for the rabbit, but there was nothing under the bush. Then I started to wonder if I would be able to find my way home, half blinded as I was.

I knew that I was straight north of the cabin, so I started walking in the direction I thought was south, stumbling along, blundering into trees and falling over rough places. I could see enough with my left eye to know that my right hand was red with blood, and each time I wiped my cheek and chin the hand got more bloody. Once I heard ducks quack nearby and thoughtlessly stopped to see whether I could make them out well enough for a shot, not realizing that in all likelihood my rifle was beyond firing. But I couldn't see farther than I could reach my arms in front of me, so I stumbled on and by some stroke of luck found the cabin.

Walter was picking a duck he had killed. Little Olive came running to meet me, and then I heard my husband cry, "Oh, my God, what happened to you?"

I let him ease me down, and then for the first time I was aware of severe pain in my right hand. I held it up and he looked quickly and mumbled, "Twenty-two shell. It's full of pieces of .22 shell. Your gun must have blown back."

He picked fragments of shell out of that hand and out of my nose for the next two days. Luckily the eye had escaped with nothing worse than powder burns; he kept washing it out with clean water. For days I had to feel my way around the cabin with the help of the other eye. Although the injured eye recovered, I never regained full sight in it.

For both of us the eleven days between May 10, when I had the accident with the gun, and the time when the ice finally went out of the Slave were a lagging nightmare of hunger and worry, mostly hunger.

Because we were so short of matches, we kept plenty of wood on hand and fed the fire at intervals all night, never letting it go out. I found a roll of wire and set snares for ducks, rabbits, muskrats, anything I might catch. In all, I snared two red squirrels and a blackbird. We peeled trees and scraped off and ate the inner bark. We pulled dead slough grass along the edge of the water and ate the tender yellow shoots below. One day I saw a fool hen, a spruce grouse, perched on the low branch of a tree. I hurried to rig a snare on a long pole, reached up, dropped it over the bird's head and jerked her to the ground. That was one of the best meals we had all that time, and for once little Olive got all the broth she wanted.

Hunger cramps kept us awake at night, and when we slept we dreamed troubled dreams of food. In my case, being seven months pregnant didn't make things any better. Right then I needed to eat for two. Each night Walter and I slept less, each day we became weaker, and the baby's whimpering for food tore both of us apart. Walter cursed himself over and over for bringing his wife and youngster down the Slave. He vowed that if we got out alive, he was through with the North for good, but I doubted that.

If only we had brought a few traps back from the tent camp, we could have caught muskrats or ducks. But we had counted on the cache of dried rat carcasses that the wolverine had robbed, and left all our traps behind.

We were down to two shells now, for my .25/35. The .22 ammunition was gone. Before that happened Walter had thrown the Stevens away to make sure I wouldn't be tempted into firing it again.

For three days our only food was what we called spruce tea. I stripped green needles off and boiled them, and we drank a few spoonfuls every couple of hours. It eased our hunger cramps and seemed to provide some strength, but a few times it also caused severe nausea.

Little Olive was no longer running around the cabin. She sat quietly and played listlessly with whatever was at hand. There was no color in her lips and cheeks, and her eyes looked hollow and dull. I can't put into words how worried and afraid Walter and I were.

We had left our fishhooks at the cabin on the east side of the Slave when we moved the previous fall, so now we made crude hooks by bending safety pins and tried fishing in the open water along the shore of the river, using pieces of red yarn for bait. Our catch totaled one very small jackfish. We had plenty of strikes, but the bent pins wouldn't land the catch. What a difference real fishhooks would have made.

On May 17 Walter killed a big mallard drake with the last shell for the .25/35, and we feasted. We even cleaned and washed the entrails, cooked them and saved them for the next day. We set aside all of the broth for the baby, and she had the first good meal she had had in many days.

The day after that I tapped a small birch tree (they were few and far between in that area) for sap. It tasted good, but we had only half a cup to divide among the three of us.

At last, at ten o'clock on the morning of May 21, the ice in the Slave began to move. By midnight it was gone and the water was rolling freely, and at three in morning of the twenty-second (it was light all night now) we shoved our clumsy boat into the river and were on our way to Bennett's.

It was dangerous to try traveling so soon after the ice went out, for chunks of stranded ice two or three feet thick and weighing many tons kept sliding off the banks and drifting down with the current. But we had no choice.

Walter rowed, and I sat in the stern and paddled and steered us away from floating ice. In our condition it was killing work, for to avoid the worst of the ice we had to stay well out from the bank and buck the current.

Our closest call came the first day. Rowing close to shore, we saw a huge block of ice come sliding off a pile forty feet high and crash into the water almost alongside us. The force of it literally lifted our rowboat into the air and sent it flying. We wound up one hundred and fifty feet out, in the swiftest part of the current, right side up only because we had happened to be pointed in the right direction when the ice thundered down.

Little Olive had the last of the duck soup that day. Walter and I drank spruce tea and gathered and ate slough-grass roots. We also drank water often because it seemed to ease our hunger, and we kept rowing until we gave out.

It took six days to make the twenty-three-mile trip up the Slave to Bert Bennett's cabin, and they were as dreadful as any days I can remember. We pulled to shore at Bennett's place at midnight on May 27, dirty, ragged, starving, and burned so black by wind and sun that we hardly recognized our own reflections when we looked in a mirror. In those six days Walter and I had eaten nothing but spruce tea, grass roots, and the inner bark of trees.

A Mr. and Mrs. King from Fort Smith were at Bennett's. They had come down on the ice in March. She gave each of us half a biscuit and a couple of spoonfuls of stewed apricots, but the food was too much for our stomachs. We awakened three hours later with dreadful cramps and were miserably sick for the next twelve hours. It was four days before I was well enough to be out of bed, but Mrs. King fed me a few spoonfuls of canned soup and cream every hour, and at the end of that time I felt fine. By then Walter and the baby had bounced back until they were as good as new, too.

Bennett and the Kings fixed us up with clothing, and we waited out a comfortable and happy month, until the *Miss Mackenzie* came up the Slave on her first trip of the year. We boarded her near the end of June, and the trip to Fort Smith was perfect.

Walter sold his furs there. He had 560 muskrat pelts, 27 mink, 3 red foxes, 4 skunks, and a few weasels. The fox pelts brought $25 each, the mink $10. The Northern Trading Company store had grubstaked us when we left for the trapline the previous August. Walter paid off the debt and had $1,060 left in cash. We agreed that we had never seen money that came harder.

We went by portage road from Fort Smith to Fort Fitzgerald and then took the stern-wheeler *Slavie,* the same boat Walter had briefly helped build a year earlier, on up the Slave, across Lake Athabasca, and up the river of that name to Fort McMurray. We were reversing the route we had traveled on our trip of hardship and danger right after the ice went out the spring before. To save money we paid our passage by waiting on tables and washing dishes.

The *Slavie* was towing two big scows, one lashed on either side, and there were some three hundred passengers crowded aboard the scows and the boat itself. They were a picturesque lot, too, mostly a mixture of white trappers coming out at the end of winter and Indians on their way to collect treaty money from the government.

Before we left Fort Smith I had gone to the R.C.M.P. post and told the story of Garvin, the old trapper who had come to our cabin in February. I was told later that the Mounties went down the Slave by boat to his place and found him there, in very poor condition, but I never learned whether the poor old man lived or died.

At Fort McMurray a doctor removed the last two slivers of .22 shell from my nose, and then we boarded a train for Edmonton, on the way to Bellingham, Washington, where Walter's family was living by that time. Our second daughter, Vala, was born there on July 18, four days after we arrived.

She was a scrawny, blue-gray baby, weighing only three and a half pounds, and for three weeks the attending doctor did not think either she or I would live. But we made it through, and Vala grew to be a healthy, pretty girl.

Walter went back to his trapline in the fall, but I had had enough of the North. I would never again winter in a trapper's shack with my two little girls if I could help it. I stayed behind in Washington, and soon got a job cooking at a camp where my brother-in-law, Ed Coreau, and his son Jim were taking out cedar poles.

I worked there until early in 1928. Walter came back from the fur country many times, but he never had a suitable place for a wife and children to live in. I still loved him very much, but I could no longer follow him into the bush when fall came and the trapline called. I understood that that call was something he could not resist, but the life of hardship was not fair to our children. The last time I saw him was just before Christmas of 1927, when he left once more for the North. Our third baby, Louis, had been born that September.

The pole camp closed shortly after Christmas, and in May I went to Vanderhoof, British Columbia. But the job I had there, looking after a small farm, lasted only two weeks. Then the farm was sold.

I had five hundred dollars saved up, enough for a stake, and I began looking for a homestead. I found exactly what I wanted, on the Stuart River, forty miles down from Fort St. James, in the mountain country of central British Columbia. The place had one hundred and sixty acres of good river-bottom land. Clearing it would be hard work, but I was no stranger to that. There were neighbors close by, a school just three miles away for the children, and I fell in love with it all the first time I saw it.

Neighbors pitched in and helped me build a small log house, and in June of 1928 I moved in with my family. There, less than a month later, my world fell apart.

One of the neighbors, Jack Hamilton, came with a telegram from the Mounties at Edmonton to tell me that Walter was dead. He had drowned in a lake on the Northwest Territories–Alberta border, when his canoe capsized in a windstorm.

I still remember raising my hand to my eyes to wipe away the fog that suddenly clouded them that day and Hamilton leading me to a chair by the kitchen table and saying, "You'd better sit down, Mrs. Reamer."

I had looked around at my three children. Olive, then six, stood wide-eyed, not quite taking it all in. Vala was playing with the little white kitten that a neighbor had given her, and Louis lay on his back, reaching for his toes. What was to become of them and me?

Little Olive leaned her head against my skirt and began to cry softly, and I felt a lump in my chest that made it hard to breathe. But that was not the time for tears. If I cried, I'd do it out of the children's sight.

"Will you be all right?" Jack Hamilton asked before he left.

"I'll be all right," I told him firmly.

All right? I wondered. I was twenty-six, a homesteader-trapper's widow with three little children, one hundred and sixty acres of brush-grown land, almost none of it cleared, a small log house, an old .30-30 Winchester—and precious little else.

11

I Had to Kill a Moose

The canoe was a thirty-foot dugout that local Indians had "given" me. They'd be along in the fall to claim payment in potatoes.

It had been hollowed out from a big cottonwood with a hand ax, but the tree wasn't straight to begin with, and the canoe had inherited the characteristics of its ancestor. Otherwise, the Indians would not have parted with it. As a result it was not only heavy and unwieldy but also so cranky you hardly dared to look over the side unless your hair was parted in the middle.

I was in the stern, paddling. Seven-year-old Olive was wedged firmly in the bow. Between us were Vala, five, and the baby, Louis, two. We were going moose hunting, and since there was no one to leave the children with, we would have to go as a family.

We were not hunting for fun. It was early summer, and the crop of vegetables I had planted in the garden was growing, but there was nothing ready for use as yet. The Reamer family was out of food.

The moose season wouldn't open until fall, but at that time British Columbia game regulations allowed a prospector to get a permit and kill a moose any time he needed one for food. I was not a prospector and, anyway, I had no way to go into town for the permit unless I walked twenty-seven miles each way. But my babies and I were as hungry as any prospector would ever be, and we had to have something to eat. I was sure the good Lord would forgive me, and I hoped the game warden would too, if he found out about it.

So that hot, windless July day, shortly before my twenty-eighth birthday, when fly season was getting real bad, I told the youngsters, "We've got to go and try to kill a moose." I knew moose would be coming down to the river on that kind of day to rid themselves of flies and mosquitoes. I had never shot one, but necessity is the mother of a lot of new experiences, and I decided I could do it if I got the chance. I got little Olive and 'Louis and Vala ready, loaded them into the big clumsy canoe, poked four shells, all I had, into my old .30-30 Winchester Model 94, and started upstream against the quiet current of the Stuart River.

It had been a little more than a year since the June day in 1928 when Jack Hamilton came to our lonely homestead on the Stuart to break the news that Walter had drowned in Leland Lake.

That was just before the start of the Great Depression, the period that Canadians of that generation still call the dirty thirties. There were no allowances for dependent children then. I knew I could get a small sum of relief money each month, maybe about twelve dollars for the four of us, but I did not dare to ask for it. Olive and Louis had come into the world in Canada, but Vala had been born in the United States, as I had. I was afraid that if I appealed for help, Vala or I or both of us might be sent back to that country. In the very first hours of my grief and dismay, I vowed I would never let that happen, no matter what. It was the four Reamers alone now, to fight a world of privation and hunger, but at least we would stay together.

Walter's trapline had never brought in much. I had known nothing but a hard life so far, but now I was thankful for it, knowing that I was more equal to the hardships that lay ahead than most women would be.

There were plenty of moose around the homestead, some deer, black bears, wolves, rabbits, grouse, foxes, mink, and muskrats. I'd become a farmer, hunter, and trapper on my own.

I had a little money on hand to buy food with. I owned no horses, but I dug potatoes, raked hay, did anything I could for my few neighbors to pay for the use of a team, and by the next spring I had managed to clear the brush and trees from a few acres of good land. Little Olive was my housekeeper, cook, and baby-sitter while I worked outside. I planted a vegetable garden and started a hay meadow. I hunted grouse and rabbits, and the first winter the neighbors helped me out with a gift of moose meat. We managed to eke out a living. It was all hard work, day in and day out. I dragged myself off to bed when dark came and crawled out at daylight to begin another day, but at least I and my youngsters had something to eat.

Then, in July of 1929, our food gave out. I couldn't bring myself to go deeper in debt to my neighbors, and that was when, in desperation, I decided on that out-of-season moose hunt. With the few odds and ends we had left, we could make out on moose meat until the garden stuff started to ripen.

We hadn't gone far up the Stuart that day before I began to see moose tracks along shore and worn moose paths coming down to the river. Then we rounded a bend, and a big cow was standing out on a grassy point, dunking her ungainly head and coming up with mouthfuls of weeds.

I had no wish to kill a cow and possibly leave a calf to starve, but I had never been more tempted in my life than I was right then. The big animal meant meat enough to last us the rest of the summer, and by canning it I could keep every pound from spoiling. I paddled carefully ahead, whispering warnings to the kids to sit still and keep quiet. The closer I got, the more I wanted that moose. She finally saw us and looked our way, while I wrestled with my conscience.

I never knew what the outcome would have been, for about the time I was getting near enough to shoot, little Olive let out a squeal of pure delight as an awkward red-brown moose calf raised up out of the tall grass. That settled it.

The children were all talking at once now, and the cow grunted to her youngster and waded out, ready to swim the river. She was only two hundred feet away at that point, and all of a sudden she decided she didn't like the canoe there. Her ears went back, the hair on her shoulders stood up, and her grunts took on a very unfriendly tone.

I stuck my paddle in the mud and waited, wondering just what I'd do if she came for us. There was no chance that I could maneuver the cumbersome dugout out of the way. But I quieted the youngsters with a sharp warning, and after a minute the cow led her calf into deep water, and they struck out for the opposite side of the river, where they waded ashore and walked up a moose trail out of sight.

A half mile farther up the river I landed and took Louis piggy-back. Then, carrying the gun, I led the way very quietly across a grassy point where I thought moose might be feeding. I didn't see any, however, and now the kids began to complain that they were getting very hungry. I was hungry, too. We sat down on the bank to rest, and I saw a good rainbow trout swimming in shallow water.

I always carried a few flies and fishhooks in my hatband, and now I tied a fly to a length of string and threw it out, using the string as a handline. The trout took the fly on about the fifth cast, and I hauled it in. I fished a little longer and also caught two squawfish. We hit back to the canoe then, I built a fire and broiled the rainbow and one of the squawfish on sticks. The kids divided the trout, I ate the squawfish. As a rule, they have a muddy flavor, and I had really caught those two for dog food, but to my surprise that one tasted all right.

A little farther up the Stuart we came on two yearling mule deer, with stubby spikes of antlers in the velvet, watching us from a cut bank, but they spooked the instant I saw them and disappeared in the brush. A little later the same thing happened with two bull moose. They saw the canoe and ran into the willows while I was reaching for my gun. I was so disappointed and discouraged that I wanted to bawl. That made four moose we had seen, counting the calf, without getting a shot, and I decided that killing one was going to be a lot harder than I had thought. And my arms were so tired from paddling the heavy dugout that they felt ready to drop out of the sockets.

I had brought a .22 along, as well as the .30-30, and a little while after that I used it to shoot a grouse that was watching us from the bank. I had about given up hope of getting a moose, and was ready to turn back for the long paddle home when I saw what looked like the back of one, standing almost submerged in the shade of some cottonwoods up ahead. I shushed the kids and eased the canoe on for a better look, and, sure enough, it was a young bull, probably a yearling. Just the right size for what I wanted.

The moose was feeding, pulling up weeds from the bottom and putting his head completely under each time he went down for a mouthful. I paddled as close as I dared and warned the two little girls to put their hands over their ears and keep down as low as they could, for I had to shoot over their heads. I put the front bead of the Winchester just behind the bull's shoulder, at the top of the water, and when he raised his head I let him have it. He went down with a great splash, and I told the kids they could rise up and look.

Luckily, the young bull did not die right there in the deep, muddy water. Getting him ashore for dressing would have been a very hard chore. When we got close with the dugout he was trying to drag himself out on the bank. My shot had broken his back. I crowded him with the canoe, feeling sorry for him all the while, and as soon as I had him all the way on dry land I finished him with a shot in the head.

I had always hated to kill anything, and by that time I was close to tears from pity for the moose. Then I saw little Olive leaning against a tree, crying her heart out, and Vala and Louis with their faces all screwed up in tears, and I felt worse than ever. But I reminded myself that it had to be done to feed the children, and I wiped my own eyes and explained to them as best I could. About that time a porcupine came waddling along, and that took their minds off the moose.

Dressing a moose, even a yearling bull, is no fun. I went at it now, and it was about as hard a job as I had ever tackled. The kids tried to help but only succeeded in getting in the way. And while I worked I couldn't help worrying about my out-of-season kill. What would happen if I were found out? Would the game warden be as understanding as I hoped?

When the job was done, I built a small fire and boiled the partridge I had shot, with a few pieces of moose meat, for our supper, giving little Louis the broth in his bottle. I felt better after I ate. I loaded the meat into the dugout and started home, but it was full dark now, and I was so tired that I soon decided not to go on.

We went ashore, spread out a piece of canvas, part under and part over us, and tried to sleep. The mosquitoes were so bad that I finally gave up. I sat over the children the rest of the night, switching mosquitoes off with a willow branch. Daylight came about four o'clock, and we got on the way again. I'll never forget that early-morning trip back to our home place. My hands were black with mosquitoes the whole way, and the torment was almost too much to endure.

Joel Hammond, a neighbor, had given us some flour that he had made by grinding his own wheat in a hand mill, and the first thing I did was build a fire and make a batch of hot cakes. The flour was coarse and dusty, but with moose steak and greens fried in moose fat, those cakes made a real good meal. Then I went to work canning meat.

That was the only moose I ever killed out of season. When hunting time rolled around that fall, I got a homesteader's free permit and went after a winter's supply of meat. It came even harder that time.

The first moose I tried for I wounded with a shot that cut through the tip of his lungs. He got away in thick brush, and I took our dog, Chum, and followed him. Chum drove him back into the river, and he swam across and stood wheezing and coughing on the opposite side, too far off for me to use my last remaining shell on him. Chum swam the river in pursuit and started to fight him in shallow water.

Another neighbor, Ross Finley, who lived on the quarter section next to mine, heard the shooting and came to lend a hand. He loaded little Olive and me into the dugout, and we paddled across to where the dog was badgering the moose. Finley used my last shell when we got close but missed, and the bull, fighting mad by now, came for the canoe, throwing his head this way and that. I was badly scared, for neither I nor Olive could swim a stroke, and I knew that one blow from the moose's horns would roll the dugout over like a pulpwood bolt.

I moved fast with the bow paddle, and the moose missed us by less than a foot as I swung the canoe away from him. He was in deep water now, and Chum was riding on his shoulders and biting at the back of his neck. The dog claimed his attention for a second or two, and I reached down and grabbed Finley's .22

that was lying in the bottom of the dugout. I shot him at the butt of an ear, with the gun almost touching him. He sank quietly out of sight, leaving Chum floating in the water. The dog was so worn out from the ruckus that he had to be helped to shore.

We went back then and tried hard to locate the dead moose, but the current carried it swiftly downriver, and it was days before it was found, lying in shallow water at the mouth of a creek, bloated and the meat spoiled.

There were plenty more around, however. They could be heard fighting at night, grunting and snorting, and sometimes their horns would clash with a noise as loud as an ax hitting a hollow log. In the early mornings I saw as many as five at one time along the weedy river shore. I waited and picked the one I wanted, and that time I killed him with no trouble.

The Stuart was full of ducks and geese that fall, and there were grouse everywhere. I had plenty of ammunition for the .22 and always a few .30-30 shells around. I canned everything I killed and no longer had to worry about a meat shortage. Life was beginning to sort itself out the way I wanted it to.

A few unmarried men came around and tried to shine up to me, but I wasn't interested. All I wanted was to get more land cleared and buy a cow or two and a team of horses of my own. The young homestead widow was proving to herself that she could take care of her family and make the grade.

12

The Long Walk

Before the spring of 1930 arrived I confronted one of the most discouraging ordeals that had ever befallen me.

By February our food was gone except for canned meat and a few cans of vegetables. We had used the last of the hand-ground flour that Joel Hammond had given me, and we were desperately in need of store-bought groceries.

I had no money, but I decided to walk the twenty-seven miles to Vanderhoof, on the Prince George–Prince Rupert railroad, and try to get our needed supplies on credit. I knew I could pay for them with potatoes the next fall, for by that time I had enough land cleared to grow a bigger potato crop than we needed for ourselves.

I left the three children with the George Vinsons, neighbors a mile and a half downriver, and started out on a cold, wintry morning. I had a road to follow, but only a few teams and sleighs had traveled it, and the walking was hard, in deep snow. Two miles out of Vanderhoof I finally hitched a ride.

I had no luck getting credit against my potato crop. Those were hard times, and the merchants couldn't afford much generosity. I tried first of all to buy badly needed rubbers for myself and the kids. They were the cheapest footgear available. But the store turned me down.

A kindly woman who ran a restaurant did better by me, however. She fed me a good dinner, and when I put her down for fifty pounds of potatoes she just smiled and shoved a chocolate bar into my pocket. She got the potatoes when the time came, anyway.

Another storekeeper said he couldn't let me have things on credit, but he gave me two dollars in cash and told me to do the best I could with it. I knew where part of it was going—for the oatmeal and sugar I had promised the children. But I could see no way to pay for another meal for myself or a room for the night, and I walked around Vanderhoof thinking of how wet and cold our feet would be in the slush of the spring thaw, about as downcast as I had ever been in my life.

Finally I decided to make one last desperate attempt. Some of my neighbors on the Stuart River traded at a store at Finmoore, nineteen miles east of Vanderhoof. I also had a friend there, Mrs. John Holter. I would walk the railroad track to Finmoore and try my luck. At the time I didn't know how far it was, and I expected a hike of only ten miles or so.

It was almost dark when I started. The railroad ties were crusted with ice and the walking was very bad. My clothing was not enough for the cold night, either. It consisted of denim overalls, men's work socks, Indian moccasins and an old wool sweater with the elbows out, worn under a denim jacket.

I had never been brave in the dark, any time or any place, and that walk was an ordeal of the most dreadful kind. All I could think of were the stories I had heard about hobos, railroad bums, and I was afraid of every shadow.

I got to the lonely little station at Hulatt, fifteen miles from Vanderhoof, at midnight, and asked the stationmaster if I could rest until daylight. I lay down on the floor by the big potbellied stove. It was warm and cozy, and I was worn out. I started to drift off to sleep, but then I began to worry about the children and the likelihood that if I was later in getting home than I had promised, they might come back to the house and get into trouble starting a fire. Things were hard enough without having the place burned down. I got up and trudged away along the track once more.

It was two in the morning when I reached the Holter place. Mrs. Holter fixed me a sandwich and a cup of hot milk, and I fell into bed. My friend shook me awake at nine o'clock, as I had told her to. Those scant seven hours of sleep were all I had in more than thirty-six.

Mrs. Holter loaned me another two dollars, and I went to the general store and struck it rich. The proprietor, Percy Moore, stared at me in disbelief when I poured out my hard-luck story. "You've walked from the Stuart River since yesterday morning," he exclaimed. "That's forty-six miles!"

"No, forty-four," I corrected him. "I got a ride the last two miles into Vanderhoof." Then I added, "I've got fourteen more to walk home before dark tonight, too."

The first thing he let me have, on credit, was the four pairs of rubbers I needed so desperately. Then he took care of my grocery list. Eight pounds of oatmeal, three of rice, five of beans, five of sugar, and, for a bonus, a three-pound pail of strawberry jam. That was a luxury I had not dreamed of. I plodded away from Finmoore at ten o'clock that morning with almost thirty pounds in a packsack on my back, but never before or since was I more happy to carry a load.

Three inches of wet snow had fallen that morning, and the fourteen-mile walk was endless, each mile longer than the one before. The pack got heavier and heavier, and sometime in the afternoon I began to stumble and fall. I was so tired by that time, and my back ached so cruelly from the weight of the pack, that

I wanted only to lie in the snow and go to sleep. But I knew better. Time after time I drove myself back to my feet and staggered on, slipping and sliding and falling again.

To this day I do not know what time it was when I reached home, but it was long after dark. Chum met me in the yard, and no human being was ever more glad to fumble at the latch of his own door. I slid out of the pack, pulled off my wet moccasins and socks, and rolled into bed with my clothes on. The last thing I remember was calling the dog up to lie at my feet for warmth.

The children awakened me at noon the next day, fed me my breakfast, and rubbed some of the soreness out of my swollen legs and feet.

When I harvested my potato crop the next fall, I paid off my debt to Percy Moore in full, except for one item. There was no way to pay him, ever, for *his kindness to me* when I was broke and had three hungry children at home.

I made many more trips to Finmoore in the years before I left the Stuart, for I did most of my trading at his store, and when times got better he and his wife and daughter often came out to our farm and bought vegetables and eggs from me. I still remember walking back to his place the next year carrying six dressed chickens, selling them for fifty cents apiece, spending the money for food, and packing it home. Three dollars bought quite a heavy load in those days, too.

Things went on about the same for us the third summer after Walter drowned. I plowed fifty acres of land for Jack Hamilton that spring. Olive and Vala were eight and seven now, and Louis, the baby, was past two. The girls cleared and burned brush for Hamilton, and we all picked strawberries and raspberries for Joel Hammond. We got more work putting up hay and digging potatoes and made enough money to buy a cow. We had lots of milk and butter after that. I also bought thirty hens, and we had all the eggs we wanted.

Wild fruit was unbelievably plentiful. Blueberries and saskatoon berries grew everywhere. The saskatoons are the service berry, Juneberry, or shadbush of the eastern United States. They were available in lavish abundance, but because they were not as tasty as blueberries, we rarely bothered with them.

Then there were bog cranberries and the wild viburnum that is commonly known as the highbush cranberry. Both of them called for plenty of sugar, but they were excellent for jellies and jams.

There were also wild strawberries and raspberries, and even gooseberries and black currants, growing in profusion. Some we canned, some we dried in the sun, some we ate as we picked them.

Our garden and the land I had cleared were producing bountifully. I sold potatoes and garden stuff and bought the groceries we needed. The Reamers were doing very well, all as healthy as young deer and just about as lively. I even built a woodshed, splitting the shakes for the roof myself, out of blocks I cut with a crosscut saw.

Before that summer was over I had the first argument I had ever had with a black bear. The bear won hands down.

I left the kids at home one day and walked two miles to Jack Hamilton's place to pick up mail and groceries he had brought out from town for me. Because I'd have enough to carry on the return trip, I didn't take the old .30-30 Winchester that went with me on most of my trips. The country along the Stuart was still wild and sparsely settled, and you never knew when you were going to meet a quarrelsome moose, wolf, or something in an unfriendly frame of mind, so I usually carried the rifle as a precaution. But that day I went without it.

When I was ready to go home I took a shortcut across the fields and through timber along the river. I hadn't walked far when I saw a bear and three cubs grubbing ants out of a rotten log at the edge of a small burn.

I had lived all my life in the woods and wasn't really afraid of bears. I had met lots of them but had yet to come across one that didn't run at sight of me. Nevertheless, I knew enough about them that I didn't think it would be wise to walk on past this family. I was fully aware that a sow with cubs is likely to be short-tempered.

"Get!" I yelled at the top of my voice. "Get out of there!"

The old bear came back with a loud woof, but she and two of the cubs took me at my word. They lit out in the opposite direction. The third cub got confused. I guess he was so busy with his ant hunting that he didn't know where I was, and he came straight for me.

The old female ran only about three or four times her own length before she looked back. She swapped ends, started after the cub, and let out a roar that fairly lifted me out of my tracks. I turned and ran for Jack Hamilton's open fields as fast as my legs could carry me, but it seemed to me right then that I had lead weights on my feet.

I looked back once, and she was gaining fast. But the cub stopped and then she stopped, and when I got out into the field she was nowhere in sight. I went back to Hamilton's house, borrowed a horse, and rode home. So far as I can remember, that was the last time, in the years we lived on the Stuart, that I ever went into the woods on foot without a gun.

I didn't guess it at the time, but that encounter marked the beginning of something, too. For many years to come, I'd have bears in my hair a fair share of the time.

When it came time to kill a moose for our winter's meat that fall (Olive and Vala had started to school by that time, in spite of a three-mile walk along the Stuart River each way), I knew exactly what to do, or at least I thought I did. I left the three kids in the house one evening when a cold drizzle of rain was falling, paddled our big thirty-foot dugout very quietly up the river to

Bear Creek, and spotted a huge bull standing in the water at the mouth of the creek.

I had to stand up in the canoe to see enough of him to shoot. My old .30-30 didn't kick much, but I couldn't help wondering what was going to happen when it went off. That heavy, Indian-made dugout would tip over if you breathed on it real hard. I finally pulled the trigger anyway, and the moose fell like a ton of bricks. Somewhat to my surprise, the canoe stayed right side up, too. But when I paddled to where the animal had dropped, he wasn't there. I looked around, saw a streak of blood leading up from the water toward the timber, and the next thing I knew a very wild-eyed and ugly moose was looking down at me from the top of the bank thirty feet away.

I dropped the paddle and grabbed the gun, but before I could get the sights on him he lifted his nose in the air and let out the worst groaning noise I had ever heard. It made every hair on my head stand on end. I shot too soon, through thick willows, and missed him. He whirled and ran, and the next I saw of him he was going along a hillside at very long range. I held the .30-30 about two feet over his shoulder and touched it off, and he bunched himself up but kept going.

I found a good blood track, but it was raining hard by then and getting dark, so I quit and went home. The next morning I put Chum on the track, and he found the moose dead not far from where I had turned back the night before. Two good shots had gone into him, one high in the shoulder, the other above a kidney and up into his ribs. The second hit was probably an accident, at that range, but, at the time, I felt pretty well satisfied with my shooting.

A 1906 photograph of the Goodwin Ranch in Withee, Wisconsin, where my parents' children were all born. My sister Ida and her husband bought the farm when my parents decided to move north.

My father packing a bear home to Tomato Creek on his back, 1916.

<

My parents, Archie and Clair Goodwin, with my brother Frank, at Thorpe, Wisconsin.

My father and my stepmother, Maggie Miller Goodwin, in a store-boughten sleigh drawn by our team, Maud and Nellie, at Tomato Creek.

My brother Lea with pelts of silver foxes we raised at Tomato Creek.

Lea with a tame deer at Tomato Creek.

My brother John, at right, milking Jule, and my brother Lea milking my cow Goldie at Moose Portage, Alberta, Canada.

My brother Frank leaving Athabasca Landing with the mail team bound for Fort McMurray in 1919. Frank served in World War I and later came home and hauled mail for the government.

Dog teams leaving Fort McMurray for down north.

Walter Reamer, our daughter Olive, O.R., and my nephew Jim.

I once stayed in this prospector's camp on the Osilinka River.

Fort McMurray, Alberta, Canada, in 1922. It was a welcome change for a young wife after her years in the bush. There were women for neighbors, children, good lively music on dance night, people coming and going beneath the kitchen window.

Steamboat on the Athabasca.

Ice along the Athabasca River.

The torn-up boats and housetops give a small indication of the awesome power of the ice moving down the river.

This house at Fort McMurray was a casualty of the ice in May 1922.

My daughters at a camp in Washington State.

...ve and Vala at a logging camp ...Washington where I worked as ...k.

Olive, Vala, and O.R. in Washington.

Vala with her horse Shorty at Stuart River in 1934.

Vala Reamer, Stuart River, 1938.

<
O.R. holding Shorty, with Vala and
dog Chum at Stuart River, 1936.

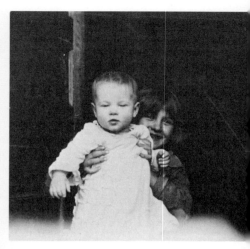

My son, Louis.

The bank where many people carved their names at Stuart River.

Louis on horseback at Stuart River in 1935.

Moose were plentiful at Stuart River though there are few there now.

A large bull moose with antlers in the velvet swimming Stuart River in July.

John Fredrickson in 1940, shortly
before we were married.

O.F., 1941.

John's family in Sweden not long before he came to Canada in 1927.
His mother, Linda, youngest brother, Thure, and father, Fredrick
August Fredrickson, are in the front. In back, Emanuel, John, Victor,
Ida, and Gustaf.

At Port Hardy on Vancouver Island in 1946.

With our catch, a twenty- and a fifty-pound salmon, on Vancouver Island.

With our dog Jeep at a Prince
George motel in 1948.

Our dog Jeep.

A prospector or trapper built this cabin we stayed in.

The door was torn half off, the one window had been broken, and the inside was a shambles. The bear had done a thorough job of ruining things.

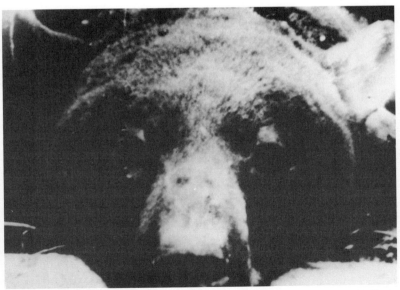

Old White-Ear, who had plagued us throughout our prospecting summer, was finally disposed of.

O.F. with moose killed at Stuart River.

At Stuart River with Jeep in 1955.

Vala and Olive.

13

I'll Always Hate Wolves

The next spring, March came in like the proverbial lion. But before the end of the month the snow squalls and blustery winds were gone, and the lion had been replaced by a fluffy white lamb. A soft chinook wind blew out of the southwest, tugging fleecy clouds across the blue sky like white sails, and rivulets of water ran everywhere.

In all the years I lived on our homestead on the Stuart, I could never make up my mind which of the four seasons I loved best. Spring brought its relief from winter and its miracle of renewal. In summer, when the fragrance of clover drifted across the fields and cattle grazed contentedly in knee-deep grass, the woods were like green cathedrals. Autumn set the earth ablaze with color, and its bright beauty was something no human could resist. Then came winter, when birch and aspen and cottonwood cast long shadows across the new snow, spruce and pine were like dark green blocks in a patchwork quilt, and the stillness pressed down until you could feel it.

I guess I never tried very hard to find one season more beautiful and wonderful than the rest. One thing they all had in common, each brought its own vexing problems as well as its own magic.

When calving time came that spring, our cow, Dixie, got into trouble, and I found myself an untrained midwife.

That cow was pretty precious to us for practical reasons, and, on top of that, she was a pet we all loved. When her time was about at hand, I got up twice in the night and went to the barn to check on her. Vala went again right after daylight, in my place. She came flying back, and I knew something was wrong.

"Mama, I think Dixie is sick," she cried.

Dixie was sick indeed. Her calf was coming hind feet first, and I knew that meant a very hard birth.

I had seen enough of such things on the homestead at Tomato Creek to know what had to be done, but I was not sure I could do it. However, I had to try.

I got Dixie on her feet and led her into a small corral beside the barn. She lay down, and I gave her time to deliver, but it was no use. I could see that she was getting weak.

I grabbed the feet of the calf and tugged each time the cow strained, but the calf would not come. By that time Olive and Louis had joined Vala and me. Children learn the ways of life early on the frontier.

The four of us rigged a chain block to one of the posts of the corral and fastened the chain to the protruding feet of the stubborn calf. When we pulled now we had four or five times the leverage of our bare hands.

"Gently does it," I warned the youngsters.

It was much like a doctor delivering a human baby with forceps, only far cruder. It took twenty minutes of agonizing labor, with poor Dixie doing all she could, and then our joint efforts brought into the world a fine heifer calf.

But the mother did not undertake to lift her head off the ground after the birth, and I could see the big veins on her udders turning blue. I moved the chain block, and we pulled her into the normal position of a cow lying down to chew a cud.

Next I skidded the wet newborn calf around in front of her, stroked it, and then ran my hand over her nose. Her eyes came open, her drooping ears lifted, and she smelled her baby in the fashion of bovine mothers from the beginning of time. Next, she tried to lift herself to her feet.

We moved the calf out of the way, and she succeeded. In another half hour everything was back to normal. Our efforts had saved both cow and calf.

A few weeks after that, toward the end of May, I climbed onto one of our horses one morning to ride six miles to an abandoned hay meadow where a man by the name of Jim Fedderly had lived long before. We called it Fedderly's Meadow. Nobody had cut the hay there for many years, and I thought we might cut and stack it to help out with our winter feeding. I left the children at home.

I had ridden about five miles when I pulled my horse up to look at some flowers beside the trail. I decided to climb off and had one foot out of the stirrup when the horse threw up his head, blasted out a frightened snort, and then I heard a strange noise almost like a growl behind me. I looked over my shoulder, and not more than fifteen feet away stood a cow moose, ears flattened back against her neck and her hair all standing up, at the point of lunging for the horse and me. No animal I had ever seen had looked meaner.

The cow lunged, I heaved myself back into the saddle, and the horse jumped so hard he almost threw me off. He didn't quite get clear. The cow clouted him on the hips with her forefeet, hard enough that his hind quarters went almost to the ground, but didn't do him any serious damage. When we were safely out of reach I looked back and could see a newborn moose calf, still wet, lying where the cow had started her rush.

The next day I rode back to the hay meadow to scout out a road into it. I tied Shorty, my horse, where he could graze on bluejoint and sat down at the edge of the timber to rest. Pretty soon I heard a moose snort on the far side of the meadow. I knew that would spook Shorty after what had happened the day before, so I untied him and climbed back into the saddle in a hurry. By that time he was crow-hopping and prancing like a purebred stallion, and when I looked across the meadow again I saw a cow moose and her calf come running out of the brush, with two big timber wolves after them.

One wolf fooled around in front of the cow, just out of reach of her front feet, and while I watched helplessly the other one went after the calf, hamstrung it with one bite and pulled it down. Then it turned its attention to the cow, diving in and grabbing her by the hind legs.

My blood was boiling, and I did my best to force Shorty across the meadow to break the nasty affair up, but he'd have none of that. He pranced and waltzed the other way, and I began to shout to scare the wolves off. They ran into the brush, and I rode a circle around the two moose, yelling at the top of my lungs, hoping I could spook those two gray devils out of the neighborhood. Then I hit for home to get a gun.

I didn't have to urge Shorty. He did his level best the whole way. I suppose he thought the moose and the wolves were all after him.

I drank a glass of milk while the two girls put my saddle on Ben, our other horse. Then I loaded the old Winchester and rode back to Fedderly's Meadow as fast as the fresh horse could go. But I had been gone two hours in all, and I was too late.

I heard the cow moose blow her nose while I was still in the timber. I tied Ben and ran as fast and quietly as I could to the edge of the open, and it's hard to put into words the sight that met my eyes.

The cow was still fighting for her calf, but there wasn't much fight left in her. Her entrails were half torn out. They dragged on the ground as she turned this way and that, trying to trample the wolves with her front feet. But she was too near death to move fast enough. The hamstrung calf still lay off to one side, helpless, where I had seen it last.

The cow's hind legs failed, and she went down on her haunches while I was sneaking from tree to tree to get within good gun range. I wanted to be very sure of hitting something when I shot.

When I reached the place I had picked, one wolf was lapping blood at the cow's flank, and the other was actually sitting on her hind quarters, his red tongue lolling out from exertion. I was so furious, while I made the last few yards of my stalk, that I gritted my teeth until they hurt.

I drew a bead on the wolf that was sitting on the moose, and when the gun cracked he flew up in the air as if a bomb had hit him. The shot tore out his whole back just behind the shoulders, and he was dead when he struck the ground.

The second one made a bad mistake. He didn't know where the rifle shot had come from, and he ran straight toward me. I kept my sights on him and let him come until he swerved broadside, two hundred feet away, to streak for the brush. My shot cut across his chest, blew a hole in him, and broke both front legs. I had to follow his blood trail for four hundred feet through rose brambles and scrub trees. He was still trying to crawl off, but he was almost dead so I let him suffer and saved the one shell I had left for the cow moose. After that was taken care of, I put the calf out of its misery with my belt ax. For a woman who disliked killing things, I had had quite a day. But I never felt the slightest regret where the two wolves were concerned. I made a vow then and there that I would shoot any wolf I laid eyes on the rest of my life if I could.

I still hate wolves. I have seen a lot of their work since, on caribou and deer and other moose, and I am convinced that they kill for fun as well as food. They run and play their victims as renegade dogs do sheep. I have known them to leave a kill, full fed, pull down the next animal they came to, and go on without feeding. If they run across a bunch of deer or caribou, they don't even take time to finish a kill. They pull it down and disable it, and go after another and another until they get tired. If there are one or two old ones in the pack, with poor teeth, they'll stay with the first kill, eat all they want, and then catch up with the rest. Every now and then the pack turns on those decrepit old-timers, too, and tears them to bits.

You don't often catch an old, broken-down timber wolf in a trap, and I doubt one ever dies of old age. I have no use for them, and of all the deviltry I have known them to be guilty of, none has ever haunted me down through the years more than the savagery of that pair in Fedderly's Meadow that spring day.

The years on the homestead passed quickly. I traded two cows and a calf for a team of horses, wild and ornery as mules, but once they were tamed down they proved a good work team, and land clearing and the rest of the work went a lot better after that.

When the fall came we had five tons of potatoes to dig, and sold them at two dollars a hundredweight. I had real money then, for the first time.

Then the man who was hauling the potatoes to a gold-mining camp at Germansen Landing, one hundred and fifty miles north of our place on the Stuart, brought back word that the mining camp wanted to hire a woman cook and would pay good wages.

The children and I hated to leave the homestead, for we had come to love everything about it by that time, but I knew the work would be easier than farming and the pay better, and Louis and the girls would have other people around them, even kids of their own ages to play with. So we sold some of our stock, left the rest with a neighbor, and got ready to move to Germansen Landing. I'd leave Olive at Vanderhoof with friends, for another year of school. She would join us at the gold camp the following spring, when school was out.

Once we made the decision, we had only four days in which to complete our arrangements and pack the few possessions we would take along. That wasn't much time, but we scurried around, and at bedtime of the fourth day everything was ready.

A friend told me many years ago that once trouble gets you by the throat, it never lets go. Certainly that seemed true in my case.

Vala awakened me in the small hours that night, coughing spasmodically. She had developed a full-blown case of whooping cough without the slightest warning. A day later both Olive and Louis came down with it, and there was nothing to do but mark time until all three of them recovered and were well enough to travel.

Vala and Louis and I finally got away around the middle of October. We hitched a ride north, but the truck developed brake troubles, and when we got as far as a desolate place called Ground-hog, thirty-five miles from our destination—it wasn't even a wide spot in the road, just woods and mountains in the middle of a big burn—the driver dropped us off with our outfit, a loaf of bread and three cans of beans, to wait for a second truck that he said would be along the next morning.

We had no tent since that would have meant too heavy a load for a woman to pack. I had rolled our bedding and the rest of our meager outfit in a piece of canvas. It would serve as a make-shift tarp in case of bad weather. However, we found a tent already up and pegged in place at Groundhog. That was a kind of halfway stopping point between the Nation River stopover and the Slate Creek mines, and some kindly soul had left the tent pitched as a shelter for travelers who might be stranded in that desolate spot. But the weather was fine, and we didn't use the tent.

There was plenty of dry firewood in the burn, and of course I had a small ax along. But I had had whooping cough along with the children, and it had left me with a touch of pleurisy. Chopping wood proved a painful chore, but I had no choice, for the snow was six inches deep and the weather cold. The children slept soundly that night, but I lay awake, worried that grizzlies might find our little camp.

No truck came the next day or the next. One went by going the wrong way, toward Fort St. James, and I flagged it down and told the driver that we were nearly out of food. He left bread and a little canned stuff, but when we did not see another vehicle by noon the next day, we rolled our bedding. I put everything on my back, and we trudged off on foot. The two kids were still weak from their sickness, and we made poor time. Night overtook us, and we went on for an hour or two by moonlight, but the children played out, so I chopped green spruce branches and laid out the bedding. The night was clear, dry wood was plentiful again, and I sat up beside the fire and fed it until the first gray hint of daylight began to show. Then I roused Vala and Louis, we ate what food was left and started on.

We had not walked ten minutes when a timber wolf howled, up on the mountain to one side of us. Another answered from the other side, and then there seemed to be wolves howling in every direction. It wasn't more than another five minutes before I saw two shadows slinking along through the brush only a short way off the road, keeping pace with us, and then I caught a glimpse of another behind us.

Shivers ran up and down my spine, and I wished fervently that we had stayed beside our fire until full daylight, but it was too late for wishing to do any good. We'd have to keep on and hope the wolves wouldn't muster enough nerve to close in. All I could think of was the way I had seen those two go after the cow moose. I was carrying my .30-30, but I didn't dare use it unless I had to, for fear shooting might provoke an attack.

We walked on for a mile and a half, and my blood ran cold every minute. Every now and then I'd get a glimpse of a shadowy form in the brush to one side or see a wolf lope across the road back of us, furtive and sinister. I was desperate with fear, and finally I told the kids that I was going to use the rifle the next chance I got. But still I held off, scared of the consequences.

The morning brightened slowly. It seemed that full daylight would never come. But at last it did, and then all of a sudden the wolves were gone. I didn't see them leave; they just melted out of sight and weren't around anymore.

A short distance farther on I found the explanation. The fresh tracks of three caribou crossed the road, heading east toward the Wolverine Mountains. The wolves had picked up the caribou scent before they reached the tracks and had taken off like hounds after a rabbit. Off to the right of the road their big footprints covered those of the caribou, going at a full run. I counted the sign, and there were seven in the pack. I shuddered to think of the horrid death that awaited the caribou when those seven caught up to them, but I couldn't help being thankful that they had pulled the pack away from the children and myself.

I guess in a wolf's book caribou are safer game than people, even a woman and two kids. In all the years I have lived in the mountains of Alberta and British Columbia, where wolves are still fairly numerous, I have never known of an authenticated case of an actual wolf attack on humans. That's more than I can say for either bears or cougars, incidentally. But it is a fairly common occurrence for a pack to follow people as they did us that morning, and if they are made bold by hunger, they'll skulk in within thirty or forty feet, too. So far as I'm concerned, that's too close.

Maybe we were in no real danger from those seven that slunk along after us for that mile and a half, but being trailed in that fashion is a hair-raising experience, and I've never been more frightened in my life. Even if they don't hurt you, they can scare you half to death. From that day on, I hated wolves more fiercely than ever.

14

Mining Camp Laundress

We finally reached the mining camp at Germansen Landing on October 25, after a hard and hungry hike. We were almost a month late, and the roof fell in.

From the place where the wolves had followed us, we had trudged through six-inch snow, making between fifteen and twenty miles the first day. I shot a fool hen out of a roadside tree about noon, and we stopped and cooked it on the spot. It didn't make much of a meal for three people, but at least it was meat and it was hot, and the walking seemed a little easier after that.

At dark that day, determined not to camp another night in the timber if we could avoid it, we reached a gold camp that was known locally as Slide No. 2. The boss invited us to come in and eat, and he didn't have to twist our arms. The food was plain but good, and we put away a hearty supper. Only little Louis had bad luck. He poured apricot juice over his mashed potatoes, thinking it was gravy. I didn't notice, and he was too shy to say anything, so he ate it anyway.

After supper, when we were full fed and rested, the boss sent us by truck the last eight miles down Germansen Creek to the camp at the Landing.

We had been due there on September 27, twenty-eight days earlier, and there had been no way to send word as to the reason for our delay. I had tried to reach the foreman by radio from Fort St. James, but the message had not gotten through. It was hardly surprising that he had hired another cook instead of waiting for me.

The job I had counted on had been filled. No second cook was needed, and there we were, stranded one hundred and fifty miles north of our place on the Stuart, with very little money, no supplies, and no job. I had never been much more discouraged in my life.

But the camp boss came through in the tradition of the North. Within half an hour after he had left us, forlorn and without even a place to sleep, a man drove up with a team and sleigh.

"Climb in," he invited us. "We've got an empty cabin where we can put you up for now, and we'll get you some firewood."

He helped us unload our few items of gear, started a fire for us in the little cook stove that stood in a corner of the cabin, and because a fire of dry wood throws out heat in a hurry, the place turned warm and cheery in a few minutes.

"I'll bring you a load of wood and some grub in the morning," the teamster said before he drove off.

We slept the drugged sleep of utter exhaustion. Our only light was a candle, and as soon as I blew it out, mice started to run across the floor, up and down the log walls, and over our bed. I had never heard so many mice in one place in my life, but I was too worn out to lie awake and listen to them. They were still playing the liveliest kind of tag all around the cabin when I closed my eyes and forgot they were there.

When we awoke hours after daylight, the mice had gone into hiding. I kindled a fire in the little stove and looked around for food supplies. All I could find was a can of coffee and part of a package of macaroni. We had coffee without sugar and macaroni without salt for our breakfast, and it tasted wonderfully good.

Before noon the teamster was back with a load of firewood. A straw boss came along. There was no one at the camp to do laundry for the men, he said. Would I like to stay on in the cabin and take that job?

Would a drowning man welcome a straw?

"Okay," the man agreed. "Make out a list of the grub you need. I'll send it down, and you can pay for it later."

I had come to Germansen Landing in part because I told myself that the work there would be lighter than on the homestead. Famous last words! Through the rest of that winter I washed and ironed clothes for three miners a day, six days a week, washing by hand on an old-fashioned washboard. Evenings I darned and mended. When I left the mining camp the following fall I was skinny as a rail, and my weight down to 107, the least I had weighed since that terrible winter back on the Slave. I tumbled into bed night after night too tired to think ahead or worry about the future.

But at least I was making good wages for those hard times. I charged twenty-five cents for a shirt, ten cents for a hand towel or a pair of socks, fifteen cents for light underwear, twenty-five cents for heavy. For patching I got five or ten cents a garment. I averaged around sixty dollars a month and sent as much as I could down to a bank at Vanderhoof.

One afternoon a hard-looking member of the crew walked in. He had quit his job, he announced, was going out to Prince George, and wanted to pick up his clean clothes. There was something about his actions that I didn't like.

A woman alone in a mining camp at that time had to look out for herself, and I knew it. There was always a loaded six-gun hidden at the head of my bed, where I could reach it in a couple of steps. I moved casually toward it now.

The miner stood first on one foot, then on the other, with his tongue pushing at his cheek. Plainly he was nervous, and so was I.

"You make much money?" he blurted finally.

"I do fairly well," I replied. "I'm able to bank a little. I just sent all I had down to the bank at the end of last week."

He studied me for a minute, looked at the phone the company had installed in my cabin, turned on his heel, and walked out.

Ten minutes later the phone rang. It was Lyn, the straw boss. "Has Baldy been to your place?" he asked. When I said yes, he added, "Is he still there?"

"No, he just took his clothes and left."

"That's good," Lyn said. "I don't think he'll come back, but if he does, don't let him in. His clothes are not all he took. He stole the whole crew's paychecks out of the bunkhouse."

The next day Lyn came by to let me know that they had caught up with Baldy and he was on his way out to Prince George for trial. I stayed closer than ever to my six-gun after that.

The winter flew by. Spring breakup brought a flood and an ice jam that had to be blasted out with dynamite. A few days after the water went down, and while ice was still heaped in huge blocks along the shore of Germansen Creek, a trapper who had wintered upstream from the camp stopped at my place and told me of a cow moose with a broken hip that he had just come across, a mile up the creek. She had probably caught a foot in a crack in ice or rock earlier, broken the hip in struggling to free herself, and was in such bad shape now that she should be shot.

"I'd have taken care of her, but I didn't have a gun with me," the trapper finished.

I couldn't bear the thought of the poor thing dying a lingering death, so I loaded the .30-30, and Vala and I strapped on our snowshoes and set off on an errand of mercy.

We found the moose where the trapper had reported her, in a deep, cuplike hollow with rock walls on three sides and a fifty-foot drop over the creek bank behind her. She was down and didn't seem able to get up, so I worked in close to make sure of killing her quickly and cleanly with one shot. On snowshoes I should have known better.

I was tightening my finger on the trigger, hardly more than her own length away, with the high bank of the creek just behind me, when she lurched to her feet, wild eyed, hair all standing the wrong way.

She made a staggering lunge. I had no room to run, and I couldn't turn or dodge on snowshoes fast enough to avoid her anyway. So I did the only thing I could do—stood my ground and drove a shot into her head. She went down so close to me that I could reach out and nudge her with the tip of my snowshoe.

I heard Vala scream, "Mama, Mama!" and all of a sudden my knees started to buckle, and I wanted to sit down and maybe have a good cry. But when I had time to think about it, I realized I had furthered my education where approaching close to a wounded animal was concerned. I had made a mistake that I knew I'd never repeat.

Spring came with a rush that year, and it seemed to me I had never seen a season more beautiful. Young silvery leaves unfolded on the trees, the hills were misted with pale new green, the sky was as blue as any sky can ever get, and wildflowers bloomed everywhere along the trails.

Then it was summer, and when August was drawing to a close I was told the gold camp would close down in September. Once more we faced a decision as to where we should go and what we should do.

I favored going back to the homestead on the Stuart and taking up where we had left off. But Olive and Vala protested. They were old enough now to earn their own living, they were pretty and fun-loving girls, and the flattery and attention of the men in the mining camp had delighted them. They were beginning to want the company of men, quite naturally, and there was nothing about the hard and lonely life back on the Stuart to appeal to them.

"We should all go to Prince George and get work in the restaurants there," Olive urged, and Vala strongly supported her.

In the end it was decided their way. Early that fall we left the mountains for the settlements. It seemed to me that the wild country I loved had never been quite as beautiful as it was in the final weeks at the mining camp. The gleaming snowcaps on the mountains had never looked so clean and white, the sky never as deep a blue, the creek threading the green valley had never seemed as silvery, never chuckled its way around the rocks in such a merry way. I realized it was only because I was leaving it all, seeing it through the emotional mist of farewell, but that didn't make the parting any easier.

We rented a house in Prince George. Olive and Vala found jobs as waitresses in a restaurant, and I went to work at a hotel. Louis was left to go to school alone.

The two girls dated, went to movies and dances, loved every minute of their new and busy life. Louis and I grieved for the mountains and the woods and hated the noise and bustle and crowds of a city even as small as Prince George. I had lived my life up to then on the frontier, and I realized I'd never be happy anywhere else.

As for income, Vala and Olive were paid twenty-five dollars a month—this was still the closing years of the hungry thirties—and my wages were less than that. By the time we paid rent and bought the clothes we needed, we were no better off for money than we had been in those lean times on the homestead.

Then one of the saddest disasters of my life descended on us. Louis, now twelve, fell sick.

He came home from school complaining of a very severe headache. A local doctor showed no real concern, and in a few days he was better. Then the terrible headache came back, along with nausea and vomiting.

He was hospitalized shortly after the new year came in, but he grew steadily worse and on the first day of February 1940, he died of what we had finally learned was spinal meningitis.

Part of me died with him.

I had grieved fiercely when Jack Hamilton came to tell me that Walter was dead, but I had thrown off that grief, in part I suppose because I had to for the sake of my children. Now the loss of Louis seemed one long sorrow that would never go away.

I remember very little of what I did for months after his death. But I do recall that Olive come home one night with her eyes shining and showed me an engagement ring on her finger. She had fallen in love with an airline captain, Alex Dome, and she told me they would be married soon. He was being transferred to Carcross in the Yukon Territory, and she wanted to be with him. I could well understand that.

A couple of months after that, Olive was a radiant bride—and less than three years later she was a widow. Alex was killed on a test flight with a new plane.

15

Big John

His name was John Fredrickson. He was a big, gentle, soft-spoken man whose friends called him Big John, and the name fitted.

He walked into my life one evening in the lobby of the hotel where I was working, before Louis became ill. What I saw was six feet of quiet, kind-looking man with as winning a smile as I could recall. I liked the whole picture, so much so that my face flushed when I thought about it afterward.

The next day, while I was outside washing windows, he came down the street and stopped to ask me if I needed help. To this day I'm sure he had no intention of giving me a hand with my window washing. It was just a well-mannered and harmless way of getting acquainted.

Big John proved one of our best friends at the time of Louis's illness and death, coming frequently to the house to chat with the girls and me, calling on Louis in the hospital, doing everything he could to show his sympathy and understanding and to ease our grief when Louis died.

For a time afterward, while I went through the blackest weeks of my grief, he remained no more than a good friend. Then, in subtle, almost shy, ways he began to let me know that his attitude toward me was changing.

We were due for a stormy courtship on one count. There was another redhead on the fringes of his life.

I saw them together one evening before he had asked me for a first date, and my cheeks burned with shame afterward at the angry surge of jealousy that flared in me. Vala and I had walked uptown that evening for a cup of coffee before bedtime, and I looked through the window of a café and saw half a dozen girls sitting around a table and John Fredrickson standing talking with them. There was a redhead in the group. I suppose she was pretty, but I found it hard in that first glimpse to admit it. John was looking down at her, and she slid over on her chair with a possessive smile and motioned him to share it with her. He didn't even shake his head. Just went on smiling down at her, but in that instant I hated her, and I never got over it. I guess women are possessive cats by nature.

"What business is it of yours if he likes her?" I asked myself hotly after I was in bed that night. "You have no claim on him. He hasn't spoken to you a dozen times." But I didn't convince myself.

The next morning I came face to face with him in the lobby of the hotel, and he stood and watched me with an amused grin. I heard him chuckle as I walked on, and I realized then for the first time that the attraction I felt for this big quiet man was not a one-side thing. I also realized that he was going to enjoy making me jealous.

I changed jobs shortly after that, going to work as ticket agent for a local airline. John Fredrickson had left town, and I did not even know where he was. Pan American Airways began flying into Prince George, and the town was crowded with strangers, many from the States. Vala's social life was everything a young girl could ask for. She was meeting all kinds of interesting men and going out dancing or to movies night after night. I had more invitations than I wanted, and most of them I refused. But now and then I said yes to a man who wanted to take me dining or dancing. The ache of losing Louis was beginning to fade, and I could enjoy life a little once more.

Vala and I went together one Saturday night to a local dance hall. I didn't guess it, but I was due for a thoroughly unpleasant experience.

A friend brought a good-looking, well-dressed stranger over to me and introduced him as a visitor from Vancouver.

"Dance?" he asked, and I nodded.

I had a bit of difficulty keeping him as far away as I wanted but didn't give it much thought.

"Where have you been hiding?" he bantered. "I've been to Prince George before, but I never saw you around."

"I haven't been hiding," I said matter of factly. "I've been working."

The dance ended, and he took my hand and led me toward the door. "Let's get a breath of air," he urged. It was a warm night and I welcomed the suggestion, and anyway, I didn't want to act like a schoolgirl on her first date. But the minute we were beyond the circle of light, he pulled me roughly up to him and tried to kiss me.

I twisted my face away and pushed him back.

"What the hell's the matter with you?" he growled.

"I don't like to be pawed," I retorted, my temper rising.

He stood for a minute, looking at me insolently. "They told me you were a waitress," he sneered. "I never saw one yet that could say no."

I had never slapped a man in my life. I had always believed that if a girl behaved herself and let her intentions be known, there wouldn't be much need for slapping. But I had never been tempted as I was right then.

He took a step toward me, and I pushed him away again with all my strength.

"You've seen one now," I cried in cold fury and turned and ran back to the dance hall.

I headed for the powder room to straighten my hair, and, to make matters worse, out of the tail of my eye I saw John Fredrickson watching me quizzically.

I knew that people were prone to jump to conclusions if a girl left a dance even for a few minutes and came back looking rumpled. I suppose that was the reason I was so pleased at what happened next.

A casual friend asked me for a dance, and in the middle of it a big hand reached out and tapped my partner on the shoulder, and a pleasant voice said, "May I?"

Released, I turned, and John Fredrickson was holding out his arms.

The top of my head came just to the knot of his tie, and I felt small and deliciously feminine. That was a luxury I had not allowed myself for a long time. I had held my first partner away. But when Big John pulled me against him he did it in a gentle and respectful way, and I went willingly enough.

We danced and talked.

"Something bothering you?" he asked quietly after a time.

"Yes," I snapped, still fuming inside.

"That man you danced with a little while ago?"

I nodded. "I don't like to be pawed," I said again.

"Know who he is?" John chuckled. "Big shot from Vancouver. They say he has a lot of money."

"They told me that too," I agreed, "but Vancouver can have him."

John arched his eyebrows. "Don't you like money?" he asked.

"Not if a man like that goes with it," I said hotly. "To tell you the truth, I've never had enough to know. But I can tell you one thing. I've never liked people because they had it or didn't."

John chuckled again and dismissed the subject with a mild "It's handy to have, though."

When the time came for the supper waltz, he and I were still dancing together, and when the waltz ended we sat down in a quiet corner with our supper trays. He offered me a cigarette, but I refused, adding that I didn't smoke.

"Drink?" he asked.

I said no to that, too, and could feel my cheeks getting hot, wondering what he would ask next. But he changed the subject.

We talked about the life the children and I had had on the homestead on the Stuart, about my moose hunting, and the wolves and the gold camp at Germansen Landing.

"Do you like to hunt?" John asked.

"All but the killing," I confessed. "I've always dreaded that, but I had to do it for a living."

"We'll go hunting together sometime," he promised.

"I'd like that," I said honestly.

The conversation swung around to John then, and he started to tell me about himself. Four years younger than I, he had grown up near a small village in Sweden and had lived there until he came out to Canada in 1927 at the age of twenty-two. He had four brothers and a sister, still in Sweden, as was his father. His mother had died before he left that country.

He had loved hunting and the outdoors as far back as he could remember, he told me. One of the biggest events he could recall was the day he had killed a capercaillie, a big black member of the grouse family, weighing twelve or fifteen pounds, with a muzzle-loading rifle when he was only eleven years old. "I was so proud for a week that nobody could touch me with a ten-foot pole," he chuckled.

He had killed his first moose at thirteen, too. When he was old enough he went to work with his father and brothers at logging. In Canada he had continued to work in logging camps and at sawmills. Machinery was his specialty, he said, and in the last few years he had put in most of his time as an airplane mechanic.

"I'll walk you home if you don't mind," John said when the time came to leave the dance.

I gave him a warm smile. "I don't mind at all," I told him.

We walked home with our boots crunching in the clean new snow, and I was happier than I had been in a long time.

Vala was not yet home when we reached the house, and it was dark inside. John reached for my keys, and I gave them to him without hesitation. He unlocked the door, walked in ahead of me, and flipped a light switch. Then he stepped back to the door, said good-night, and was gone. I went into a dark room and watched him walk away. He had not said he'd ever see me again, had not asked for a date, and I was disappointed. Most of all, I guess, I was disappointed because he had not kissed me good-night. I could hardly remember back to the last time a man had done that, and from him I would have welcomed it.

He had told me that he was going north in the spring to prospect for gold and would be gone for three months. That, I told myself, would mean a lonely summer for me.

But the very next day word reached me that he had taken a job with Pan American, and my worries ended on that score. I still had the redhead to think about, however, and I was reminded of that a little unpleasantly a few evenings later when I went to the café where Vala was working to help her with the rush of customers that came in when a CNR train stopped for a forty-minute supper layover. I was busy serving when the talk of three local men caught my attention. What they were saying was not intended for my ears, but they had been drinking and were talking louder than they realized, and I could not help overhearing every word.

"I wonder if that girl that's helping Miss Vala is the one Big John was telling me about," one remarked. "I don't know what's the matter with the damned fool that he don't go after her. That redhead he's hanging around is just no good."

"The most you can say for her is that she's dynamite," one of the other men agreed. "She's stuck on herself, and she's as hard-boiled and wild as they come. But she's got the face and figure. I guess she'd be hard for a man to walk out on."

I felt as if someone had twisted a knife in my heart. That night I didn't wait for Vala to finish work so we could walk home together, as I usually did. I went by myself, hurt but also angry at my own feelings.

"Why should you care if John Fredrickson is hanging around another redhead?" I asked myself crossly. But I didn't seem able to give myself a really convincing argument.

When I got home I took a long look in the mirror, woman fashion. I finally concluded that I liked what I saw. Dark brown eyes, shining curly hair that still had plenty of auburn fire in it when the light was right, a skin as smooth as satin, pink cheeks that needed no rouge, and a figure that at least was nothing to be ashamed of. I'd give John's redhead a run for her money, I decided. I'd even resort to a little deliberate flirting and see what that would accomplish.

Vala went out to a birthday party the next evening, and I was eating supper by myself and not enjoying the prospect of a long and lonely evening, wishing some man, almost any man, would come by and invite me to go dancing, when there was a knock at the door.

I swung it open, and Big John was standing outside. He came in and we sat and talked for an hour, and then he took me by the hand and pulled me to my feet. I felt his hand move along my bare arm to steady me, and for a fleeting minute I let myself think how wonderful it would be to have this big and gentle man take care of me the rest of my life.

I felt his hand tighten ever so slightly and saw the pulse racing in his throat, and then he tapped me teasingly on the end of the nose and asked, "Why the sigh?" I hadn't even known I had sighed.

We walked out to the edge of town hand in hand, and on along a trail that crossed a small creek on a swing bridge. We didn't talk much, but it was a happy evening, and I crept into bed that night without a thought of my rival.

The next morning I had good news. A telegram came to announce that Olive, living now in Vancouver with her husband, had a baby boy. The pioneer widow was a grandmother. I'll confess I didn't feel like one.

John had one habit that was strange. He never made a date with me. He'd say, "I'll see you," or, "One of these times we'll go hunting together," but he never named the time, and I never knew exactly when he would show up. He seemed to take for granted that he'd find me at home waiting and that he'd be welcome. He was always right on the latter count, and most of the time he was right on both.

I was loafing in bed one warm Sunday morning toward the end of May when he knocked. I threw on a robe and flew to the door. John took me by the shoulders, turned me around, and gave me a little push. "Go get some clothes on, sleepyhead," he ordered. "I'll put us up a lunch. Let's make a day of it."

We walked down an old railroad grade that followed the Fraser River for a mile or so, then climbed to a hilltop where we could look out over the river and the town. We sat there and ate our lunch and talked, mostly about what was behind us in both our lives.

When we left we followed a deer trail that led toward the local airport, walking quietly. We came to an abandoned field grown up with a few pines, and just as we reached the edge of it, John stopped suddenly and pointed ahead. He whispered a warning "Shhh," and then I saw a black bear walking out into the opening trailed by two cubs.

We were hidden in brush, and for the better part of an hour that bear family put on as entertaining a show as I had ever watched. There was no warning that it would end in a dreadful and almost unendurable tragedy.

I was a trifle uneasy, for I knew enough about bears to be aware that they are forever unpredictable and untrustworthy, and I also knew that a female with cubs along can explode in red-eyed rage like blasting powder letting go. But John whispered that the way the wind was blowing there was no chance the mother could get scent of us, and as long as we stayed down in the brush out of sight, she wouldn't know we were there.

The she bear started to tear an anthill apart, and the two cubs joined in. One was either a natural-born clown or just plain awkward. He kept bumping into the other cub, and they got into an argument that wound up in a battle royal. The sow tolerated that for a minute or so, then broke it up by swatting one of the youngsters on the behind hard enough to send him flying six feet through the air.

He landed headfirst against a stump, shook his head a few times, patted one ear with a paw for all the world like a human kid who's been cuffed, and then sat very quietly for a while and thought things over. The second cub was back eating ants by that time.

Stump-Bumper, as I was calling him to myself, finally decided to make up. He started to make a queer little noise that sounded as if he were trying to whine with his mouth full of bubbles, edged up to his mother and nuzzled her on the lips and chin. All the while his little rear end was going round and round in a laughable twist.

Plainly this was a request of some kind, and the second cub teamed up with him. The she bear ignored them for a while. Then she smelled each in turn and walked a few steps to the foot of a small pine. They kept pace with her, hooking their forepaws into the fur of her belly and hopping along on their hind feet.

At the tree she sat down, leaned her back against the trunk for comfort, and let them stand upright in front of her and suckle. The whole thing had been a beautiful bit of family behavior.

There is something almost humanly tender about the sight of a she bear suffering her young to feed at her breasts. John and I watched entranced. Now and then we stole a glance at each other, our eyes sparkling with delight at the spectacle. We knew it was one humans rarely get to see. I tucked my hand into his and felt a little shiver of pleasure run through me. He squeezed my hand in understanding, but he did not move toward me or even lay his arm across my shoulder. I decided that he had never forgotten what I had said to him in the beginning about not liking to be pawed. The way I felt about him now, I wouldn't have disliked it at all, but I couldn't very well tell him that.

The two cubs finished their meal in ten or fifteen minutes. One rolled aside, curled into a ball, and went to sleep. The other kept his claws hooked in his mother's hair and lay with his head fallen sidewise. The she bear looked sleepy, too.

Then suddenly her head jerked up, she turned to face the wind, and we saw her sniff at some stray ribbon of scent. John put his lips against my ear and whispered, "It's time we cleared out."

We had half turned to sneak silently away when there was a swift and violent commotion, and the she bear went racing across the little opening at top speed, with the two cubs trailing her. In the brush at the far side of the clearing we caught a glimpse of a doe and small fawn running for the brush. They had come into the open and all but blundered head on into the bears.

There was a wire fence ahead of them, bordering the airport. The doe turned and fled alongside it, but the fawn failed to see it. He struck it hard and bounced back literally into the arms of the bear. There was one long, agonized bleat; then the bear sank her teeth into the fawn's head. John and I were close enough to hear the crunch of bones.

I had seen more than I wanted to see, and it seemed likely that if she got wind of us right then, she'd be in a very dangerous frame of mind. So we played it safe. As she started back to her cubs, carrying the dead fawn in her jaws, we crept off through the brush.

In all the years I have spent in the woods, that was the only time I have ever seen a bear make a kill. She had done it quickly and cleanly, with none of the tearing and tormenting I had watched wolves inflict. But it was a horrid thing to witness.

We walked away single file until we were safely beyond the attention of the bears. Then we stopped, and I turned and leaned my head against John's chest and let the tears flow freely down my cheeks.

"I'll never forget this day," I sobbed.

"It's too bad you had to see the end of it," he said gently. Then he turned my face up and kissed me for the first time. It was a long hard kiss, and all the hunger and loneliness of the long, hard years of my widowhood went into my response. When he would have let me go, I clung to him and kissed him again and again.

"I'll make you love me," I whispered fiercely to myself.

16

"You Could Come Along If You Wanted To"

John and I walked the rest of the way home in silence. I was too shaken to talk, and he seemed to have nothing he wanted to say. Had he already declared himself further than he intended, I wondered.

I changed from my hiking clothes into a skirt and blouse, and we went to the café where Vala worked, for a late supper. While we ate, we told her of the day we had had and the bear encounter, and when she was through work the three of us walked home together. We were almost to our house when John's redhead came strolling down the street and confronted us. The meeting seemed accidental enough, but I suspected she contrived it intentionally. We stopped to speak with her.

She ignored Vala and me as if we weren't there, tucked her hand through John's arm, and said in the sweetest possible way, "Walk me home, will you, John?"

He smiled down at her, dismissed Vala and me with a casual "See you later," and walked off with her. I could hardly believe my eyes.

We went on into the house, and I let my temper go. I called

137

the girl names I wouldn't have thought of ordinarily. Finally I ran out of words and my tantrum subsided. My daughter said very gently, "You think a lot of Big John, don't you, Mom?"

"No, I don't," I flared. "I hate him."

Vala grinned at me. "I know," she nodded. "The way you hate him sticks out all over you." Then she added, still grinning, "He'd been nice to you all day, maybe he thought he ought to be nice to her for the evening."

"Well, she can have him from now on," I said, still furious. "I want all of a man's love or none of him at all."

Vala sobered. "Oh, so it's like that," she said thoughtfully.

"It's like that," I told her, "but right now I don't know what to think."

She walked to me and put her hands on my shoulders. "Our dad has been dead a long time," she said. "You've been terribly alone and you've worked terribly hard. If you can be happy with Big John, go out and get him." Then she added, with a warm smile, "It will all come out right."

She was right. Big John came back to me as if nothing unusual had happened. A couple of evenings after that, he walked me home, and when I went to the window and stood with my back to him, looking out into the darkened street, he followed and laid his hands on the windowsill on each side of me, imprisoning me between his arms. I turned my face up to him, and he kissed me long and hard—too long. I tried to duck down to get out from between his arms, but he held me prisoner for another minute. Then he dropped his hands and let me go.

"Let's go fishing tomorrow," he proposed.

"Fine," I agreed. "But it's Vala's day off. Let's take her along."

John threw his head back and laughed. "Not going to chance it alone with me in the bush?" he asked.

"I don't think so, John. Maybe it's better not to," I told him candidly.

He and Vala and I drove out the next day to a small, remote lake a mile off the road, found an old leaky boat turned upside down on the shore, shoved it into the water, and climbed in. One of us had to bail fast enough to keep the boat afloat, but we took turns while the other two fished. I had always enjoyed fishing, and that was one of the best days I could remember. That little isolated lake crawled with trout, running around three or four pounds apiece, and we caught them about as fast as we could get our lines into the water. John was having so much fun that I think he forgot he had Vala and me along. I learned in later years that when John Fredrickson was hunting or fishing, his concentration was total. He shut out everything around him, and if he had companions, even in a canoe or boat, he was hardly aware of their presence.

He finally lost a big trout when it threw the hook at the top of the water, and for a minute I thought he was going to jump in after it. The leaky old boat rocked dangerously, and I said mildly, "John, I think you'd better take us to shore before we all drown. You'll do better by yourself."

He agreed, a bit absentmindedly, and Vala and I sat on the shore and watched him fish until he had his fill of it. While we waited, a yearling bear came along and amused us by tearing a log apart to look for ants, only a couple of hundred feet away.

When John was through fishing he came ashore, we put the few trout we wanted into a wet sack (we had released the rest as we caught them), went back to the highway, and headed for another lake that had a clean sand swimming beach.

John went one way from the car, Vala and I the other, and behind a thicket of brush we changed into our swimming suits. It was the first time John had seen me with so little on, even though swim gear covered a lot more in that day than it does now, and if I do say so, I was quite a nice eyeful. So was Vala.

We met him at the beach, and he was still talking to himself about the trout fishing. All of a sudden he stopped, measured both of us up and down with his eyes, and let out a low "S-a-a-y!" Then his eyes came back to me, and he didn't seem to notice Vala much after that, young and pretty as she was.

We had a wonderful lazy swim, and as we waded ashore at the end of it John took my hand and walked with his lips close to my ear. "I've got to have you for keeps, my darling," he said just above a whisper.

It wasn't quite a proposal, and I didn't answer him, but from that minute on I never doubted that I was his girl and he was my man.

I told myself laughingly that night that I might as well expect the rest of my courtship, and the rest of my life for that matter, to be linked with fishing and hunting and the outdoors. But those things had lain at the heart of my life up to that day, and I didn't want it any other way.

The remainder of our courtship was tempestuous, with risks I suppose I invited even while I feared them.

My love for Walter Reamer had been the love of a girl of nineteen, sweet and intense and wild. My love for John was the love of a mature woman, deep and tender and compelling beyond all restraint. Who can say which is the more beautiful to live through?

This was also the love of a woman yearning honestly to be loved in turn by a decent man. I had been a widow through the prime years of my life, and for all the hard work that had occupied me and kept me too tired to admit my own loneliness, I had had more than enough now of living alone, of stifling the hungers of both flesh and spirit that welled up in me with greater and greater insistence.

I reached the point where I was almost afraid to kiss this big quiet man, for the fire he kindled in me. And I knew the feeling was not one-sided, either, for when we were close together I could see the pulse quicken in his throat and feel his shoulders trembling within my arms.

The other redhead didn't let go without a fight, but she never really had a chance. I learned afterward that she had boasted openly that I'd never marry Big John since that's what she intended to do herself. It takes two to make an agreement of that kind, however, and in this case it would have taken three. John was right for me and I was right for him, and we both knew it.

He took me fishing again a week or two after the day he and Vala and I went, this time to a lake that had big lake trout. That was another day of wonderful fun. We caught six trout, the smallest a six-pounder, the biggest weighing sixteen. But again, as long as we fished, John didn't seem to remember that I was along, and I finally concluded that he had forgotten where he was, let alone who was with him. It exasperated the woman in me a little, but then I grinned and reminded myself that if he were the kind of man who didn't enjoy fishing, I wouldn't have fallen in love with him in the first place.

He came to the house the first thing the next morning, with unwelcome news.

"The airline is sending me up to Tacla Landing," he told me. "They've got a job up there they want me to do. I just found out about it half an hour ago. I'll be gone a month or more. Russ Baker is flying me up."

Baker was a local bush pilot, a good reliable man. I had no misgivings on that score. But Tacla Landing was a remote and lonely little outpost on the east side of Tacla Lake, in roadless bush two hundred miles northwest of Prince George. Big John might as well have been leaving for the moon.

He didn't give me much time to think about it, however. "I have to leave in two hours," he told me.

I went back with him to his room and helped him pack the few possessions he would need. Then at the last minute we stood wordless, looking at each other. I was fighting back tears, dreading the lonely weeks ahead. He reached out and pulled me close, holding me so tightly it hurt.

"Wait for me, darling," he said. "I'll be back, and I'll look after you from now on."

Still not the words I wanted to hear, still not, "Marry me now, this morning, and come with me."

I wanted to cry out, "Take me along, John. I can't bear to be away from you another day, another night!" But I had not been brought up to believe that a woman proposed, much less propositioned, and it was too late in life to change my thinking now. I choked back the eager impetuous words, and my tears with them.

I went out to the airfield with him and watched the little bush plane lift off the runway, bank, and turn on its course, watched until it shrunk to a speck in the sky over the endless, wild mountain country to the northwest. Then I went back to my job at the ticket office, praying silently that work would help fill my lonely days until the man I loved came back to me.

Two weeks went by without a letter from him, but that was not surprising. Mail contact out of a place as isolated as Tacla Landing would necessarily be infrequent.

A letter came from Olive, who was now living in Montreal. She was expecting a second child and wanted Vala to leave Prince George and come to Montreal to stay with her until the baby arrived. Vala packed and left quickly, and I was more lonely than ever. I asked for the privilege of working overtime, to fill the endlessly long and empty hours of the evenings. I'd go home an hour or two before midnight, exhausted from a long day, only to toss and turn for hours before sleep came, and then I'd dream of John Fredrickson and wake up in tears.

At last the letter came from him that I wanted so much. But it failed utterly to bring me the comfort I had hoped for. The job he was doing was bigger than he had expected, he said. He'd be away at least two more months, maybe longer than that.

Apart from that, it was a tender letter, the kind a woman would want her lover to write. He missed me terribly. He couldn't endure the separation but for the fact that he was driving himself mercilessly, working long days and falling into bed at night so tired that he was asleep in minutes. I envied him that sleep with an angry envy. Loneliness and desire worked a different magic in a woman, I thought bitterly.

Another two weeks, and then there was another letter. And this time my heart soared when I read it. My man had finally had enough of being away from me, had come to feel the same intolerable emptiness that possessed me.

"Russ Baker is flying up to Tacla the 19th of October," he wrote. "Bringing a couple of PAA inspectors. You could come along if you wanted to. There's a Justice of the Peace here, and we could be married."

If I wanted to! I laughed through tears of happiness at the roundabout proposal I had finally won from this soft-spoken suitor, and then I went to the phone and gave the airline notice that I was quitting my job. Next I started packing.

The letter had come on October 17. I had the rest of that day and one more to make my preparations, and I wanted a woman's kind of wedding, even though the setting was only a rough little outpost beside a mountain lake.

I went downtown the first thing the next morning to buy myself a wedding dress and the rest of an outfit that I thought would make John Fredrickson proud of his new wife.

I chose an ankle-length wedding gown of beige satin with silver overlace, silver slippers, and a short wedding veil with a wreath of pink and white roses. I was determined that this should be a wedding Tacla Landing would remember. (In all likelihood it would be the first one they had ever had an opportunity to remember.)

I still recall that flight as vividly as if it had happened last week. Most of the October color was gone from the trees now, but there was still some yellow on the birches and aspens, and the mountains and valleys and lakes rolled away in muted tones in all directions, like a giant tapestry so beautiful it stung the eyes.

I sat quietly in my seat as the little bush plane droned on, thinking back across the years to the life that lay behind me, the hunger and hardships of the trapline, the swift turning of the seasons on the Stuart, the first moose I had killed there, the wolves along the road to Germansen Landing, and all the rest of it.

I let my thoughts run ahead, too, as I suppose every woman does on the eve of her marriage, to the life I was going to as John Fredrickson's wife. What would it hold?

I had no misgivings. "I'll look after you from now on," John had said the last time we were together, and I believed him.

Our wedding was a bigger affair than I had expected. A nearby gold camp had closed out, and the crew had come to Tacla Landing, swelling the population almost to settlement size. In a frontier place of that kind, a wedding was a social event that nobody wanted to miss, and invitations were taken for granted.

Our bush plane landed about two o'clock in the afternoon. Two hours later, even before my future husband was home from his work, to my astonishment I was being entertained at a bride's shower.

The wedding itself was all I had wanted it to be. John and I were married in the early evening of that same day. He was proud of me and I was proud of him and we made no effort to hide our feelings or the happiness we felt at being together after our weeks of separation.

Afterward, the wife and daughter of the justice who had married us, a Mr. Alkin, entertained us at a wedding supper and dance. Getting married on the frontier was not so different from getting married anywhere else, I reflected.

I had neither expected nor wanted a life of idleness as John's wife, but neither had I expected my work to begin quite as quickly as it did. The very next day the Pan American Airways men working at the landing found themselves without a cook, and John came home and asked me matter-of-factly if I'd mind cooking for them. I told him I didn't mind, and I meant it. I was too happy to mind anything.

It would be foolish to pretend that a healthy young widow who remarries is not enchanted by her second honeymoon. She has lived enough to understand the great wonder of loving and being loved, she has lost enough to sharpen her appreciation of every minute of this rich new life, she has regained enough to realize the wisdom of savoring each day as it passes.

I was no exception. Nowhere on earth could I have found a man more gentle and tender than John Fredrickson. His every gesture toward me, his every caress, was that of a husband who adores the woman he has chosen and thinks her the most priceless possession he will ever own. Is there a deeper hunger in a woman's heart than the wish for that kind of love?

I had put my hand in John's, ready to walk with him the rest of my life. Everything told me it had been a right decision.

For two weeks we lived and moved in a daze of ecstasy and delirious happiness. But my life had never been one of continuous sunshine, and even this blissful time was to suffer an incredible interruption.

At the end of the two weeks a bush plane flew in one afternoon from Prince George, bringing mail.

There was a long official envelope addressed to me, from a court there. I opened it with a puzzled frown and found it hard to believe what it said.

"I regret to inform you," the judge had written me, "that you are not the legal wife of John Fredrickson. The papers governing your marriage were not in order, and the Justice who married you lacks the authority to marry."

I read it twice, and a wave of shame and humiliation flooded over me. I suppose it was a silly reaction, but we are all prone to believe what we have been brought up to believe, and the thought that I had been living for two weeks with a man who was not my husband robbed me of my pride and happiness as if a curtain had been drawn.

My first reaction was to go back to Prince George on the same plane that had brought the letter and wait there for John to come to me and make our relationship legal by a second marriage. He came home from work, and I poured out my tearful story to him, and he pulled me close and kissed my tears away. Then he laughed at me.

"Look, my darling," he said, "we've been living together for two weeks. In two more my work will be done and we can go out and be married properly. It won't hurt either of us to live in sin that much longer, and this is too perfect to spoil. Let's just go on pretending we are married until the job is finished."

My newfound friends all sided with him. Two weeks or four as his wife, what difference did it make, they argued. Our mistake had been an honest one, and what had already happened could not be undone.

In the end I stayed, but for me the honeymoon was spoiled. I, who had been such a warm and ardent bride, turned shy toward John now and had to fight down a wish to avoid him. I felt cheapened and ashamed by all that went on between us, and more than once when I was by myself I cried at the turn things had taken.

I know now that it was immature, schoolgirl behavior, but at the time I couldn't help it.

We lived on, "in sin," as John laughingly called it, for two more weeks. Then his work was finished, and a month to the day from the time I had arrived at Tacla Landing we flew back to Prince George.

Olive and Vala had come from Montreal for the second wedding, and it was even nicer than the one at the Landing had been. We said our vows before a minister this time, and when the service was over and I was legally John Fredrickson's wife at last, on November 22, 1941, the clouds rolled away for me as if they had never existed.

The cruel, hard years of my life were behind me now. John had promised, not once but twice, to love me and cherish me, and he was as good as his word. But if the hard part was done, there would be no lack of fun and excitement and adventure in the years that were left.

17

Back to the Stuart

The first year of our marriage went swiftly by. We spent part of it in Prince George, where John still worked for Pan American, but World War II was building to its terrible climax by that time, and in the summer of 1943 the airline sent John to Seattle for special training in engine maintenance. We lived there for two months, a time so relaxed and pleasant that John called it our second honeymoon.

We returned to Prince George in the early fall, with John confronting two weeks of vacation. We both knew what we wanted to do. We had had all we could endure of city and town. We were hungry for the mountains, the rivers, and the woods. We packed a camping outfit and hit the road for the Stuart River upstream from the homestead where my children had grown up. We'd camp and fish and loaf, and at the end of our stay, moose season would open and we'd put in a day or two hunting.

We traveled by boat, taking our time. The fishing was superb and wildlife fantastically plentiful. In a twenty-two-mile stretch of the river we counted thirty-one moose. Fly season was not

148

entirely over with, and bulls, cows, and calves were coming to the river both to feed and to escape the insects.

John was fishing from the shore one afternoon, standing at the water's edge below a high cut-bank, when there was a sudden commotion, and a mule deer doe came bounding down the bank at top speed with her fawn at her heels. She pulled up short when she saw John only a few yards away, but she didn't run. Then we saw the reason. A big, coal black timber wolf raced into sight at the top of the cut bank, only three or four jumps behind the two deer.

I yelled at the top of my lungs, and the wolf spun and vanished in the brush like a black streak. The doe and fawn turned in the opposite direction and bounded off. They ran past me only two or three steps away, plainly far less afraid of humans than of the wolf.

That was one time when we saved the lives of two deer, and John and I both felt good about it. John had his rifle along, but it was out of reach in the canoe. That was all that saved the wolf from a fatal accident. I had vowed years before to kill any wolf that gave me the chance, and the sight of that one on the heels of the doe and her fawn had fanned all my old hatred for the whole wolf clan.

We loafed up the Stuart as far as Dog Creek. On the way, we poled our boat through shallow water around a place called Big Island and watched one of the great wildlife spectacles of this continent. The spawning season of the spring or chinook salmon, biggest of the five kinds of Pacific salmon, was at hand, and the Stuart was crowded with their migrating hordes running upstream to spawn on the gravel bars and die.

Great fish, some of them weighing twenty-five pounds and more, fanned steadily up against the current, threading their way through tangles of river weed, the dark backs of many of the males tinged with dull red.

Alaskans will tell you, only half jokingly, that when a heavy salmon run is present, you can walk across a stream on the backs of the fish without getting your feet wet. That is not quite true, but it is less of an exaggeration than it sounds. A run of humpbacks will fill a pool three or four feet deep, on a clear gravel-bottom stream, so densely that the bottom cannot even be glimpsed, and many of the fish swim with their backs half out of water. In the case of those salmon that turn vivid red at spawning time, which some species do, the sight of such a pool is unbelievably alive and colorful.

The springs do not congregate in such numbers, at least in the Stuart—they are close to one thousand miles from the sea by the time they get there—but the outdoors has few sights more stirring than a school of those great dark fish, destiny-driven, pushing on against the down-rushing water, closer and closer to the mountain snows that feed the tiny creeks, leaping falls, surging through the white foam and green slicks of rapids, moving against all obstacles to the final act of their lives.

John and I could have filled our boat with them, but we did not stop to fish. We had been living on trout since the trip began, and salmon that have traveled far in fresh water are not the firm, red-fleshed fish of the ocean. To us these were not worth catching for food.

We found Dog Creek full of spawning springs, and a band of Indians camped at its mouth, drying fish, and also shooting and drying moose for their winter's food supply.

They were from Fort St. James on Stuart Lake, but one of the families was the same that had helped me dig potatoes on the homestead down the Stuart years before. We stayed and talked with them for a couple of hours.

The whole band was doing well at the harvest of their wild crops. They had hundreds of salmon split and hung on pole drying-racks, and on the way up the river we had seen several places along the shore where they had killed a moose, camped, built a rack for the strips of meat, and stayed until it was dry. It would take more than one trip with their dugout canoes to haul the fish and meat back to their homes, and they were beaming at their good fortune.

We turned back at Dog Creek, letting the steady current of the Stuart take us along on the return trip. We had brought no motor for our small rowboat, and it was pleasant to drift downstream for a change. That afternoon we witnessed one of the most unusual incidents I have seen in my lifetime in the woods.

We rounded a bend, and at the shore a quarter mile ahead two bald eagles were diving savagely at a young mule deer.

The deer was a spikehorn buck, probably a yearling, to judge by its size and velvet-coated antlers, small but still far too heavy for the eagles to carry off. Astonishingly, however, it apparently was not too big for them to kill, and they already had it conquered and reduced to helplessness. Maybe they had surprised it drinking at the river's edge and stunned it sufficiently with the first blow they struck that it could neither escape nor fight them off.

It was running this way and that now, confused, circling, stumbling to its knees, backing into brush and logs, rearing on its hind legs to strike out with its forefeet but no longer agile enough to make the blows count. The eagles dived on it one after another, always striking for its head. Through the field glasses I was carrying I could see them drive home their great yellow feet, closed like mailed fists, and I could also see that the head of the deer was torn and bloody.

As often as one eagle struck, it would zoom up in readiness to stoop again, while the second streaked down like a feathered rocket.

In a battle of that kind, John's sympathies and mine have always been with the underdog. He had reached for his rifle and laid it across his knees, and he was driving the boat ahead with all the strength he could put into the oars.

"We're going to be too late, John," I told him. "They'll finish him before we're close enough to shoot."

"Put your glasses down and try a shot anyway," he urged. "Maybe it will scare them off. Shoot to one side, so you don't hit the deer."

I took the rifle and fired quickly, aiming for the opposite shore of the river. If the eagles even heard the whiplash report of the gun, they gave no sign. They came at the deer again before the last echoes had rolled away, and now they knocked it off its feet, and it could not get up.

"He's down," I cried, "and they're standing on him. They'll peck the poor thing to death!"

John rammed the nose of the boat against the muddy shore, grabbed the rifle out of my hands, reached the brush-grown bank in one long jump, and ran for the scene of the fight. I took time to tie the boat to a tree before I raced after him.

The sight of humans on foot was too much for the eagles. They left the deer, but they made it plain that they were not giving up their kill just yet. They circled a time or two above the river, their wild and angry screams ringing down to us. Then they planed down and landed in a dead tree only a hundred yards or so away.

John was breathing hard from his run along the bank. He took a couple of steps to a small aspen, laid the rifle in a fork, and at the crack of the gun one of the big white-headed birds spun to the ground, turning slowly like a falling leaf. The other flew off, and we ran for the deer again.

It lifted its head when we came up to it, but its neck was twisted sidewise and it seemed dazed. If it saw us, it was too near death to show fear. Its tongue hung out from exhaustion, and its whole body was quivering.

Anyone who believes that the natural world is other than a

place of claw and fang should have watched that merciless attack.

I ran my hands over the torn, bloody head. I had once done enough nursing in a Washington hospital to have some knowledge of head injuries, and I could feel no evidence of a broken skull. But those powerful, airborne blows had knocked it out, and it acted much like a human who has suffered a concusssion.

I wet my handkerchief in the river, washed the blood off the deer's head and neck, and wrung cold water onto its tongue and into the side of its mouth.

"Let's make camp here and see if we can pull him through," I suggested. John was more than willing.

He went after the boat, we got the tent up, and I went on wetting the deer with cold water and squeezing water into its mouth. At dark it still lay where it was, but the tired body no longer quivered, and its tongue was back where it belonged.

When daylight came, it was still in the same place, stretched out as if dead, but its flanks were rising and falling in the steady rhythm of breathing, and when I walked to it and touched it with my toe it flinched and its eyes widened.

"He's going to make it," I predicted to John.

We were finishing breakfast when the surviving eagle came up the river, flying high over the trees as if looking for its kill. It alighted on a bare branch of the same tree from which John had shot its mate the day before, and he stepped quietly away from the breakfast fire and picked up his rifle. His shot hit the big bird dead center, and it fell like a stone.

At the report of the rifle the deer winced hard, and I felt more confident than ever that it would live.

I gave it water from a spoon and cup the rest of the morning. John finally picked it up as if it had been a helpless calf, carried it to the boat, and laid it in the bottom. We took down our tent and started downriver to our main campground. By now I had given the little buck the name of Tannie, for its tan color, and was thinking of it as a pet deer.

It lay beside us in our tent that night, but when I awoke at daybreak it had righted itself into the normal position of a resting deer, its head was up, and it was looking alertly around at the strange surroundings.

While John got the breakfast fire going, I coaxed and pushed the deer down to the edge of the water. He lowered his head with difficulty because of the cuts and wounds along his neck, but at last he drank, long and deeply, wandered a short distance down the shore and nibbled at the weeds and grass that grew higher than his belly.

We went fishing after breakfast, and he lay quietly on the bank and watched us.

"He's adopted us," John told me.

We caught a couple of good Dolly Varden trout and a rainbow, went ashore, and ate a hearty meal of fish, with the deer resting only a few feet away, chewing his cud contentedly. I knew that British Columbia game regulations would not allow us to keep him as a pet, and I was beginning to wonder how to go about getting rid of him.

But late in the afternoon that problem solved itself. John started to gather wood for our supper fire. He picked a dead poplar, and with the first loud "Thwack" of the ax against the dry trunk, Tannie bounded for the brush in proper wild-deer fashion.

We saw no more of him for three days. Then we spotted him in company with a large doe and young fawn. We got close enough to make out the injuries on his head and neck before the doe blasted out a warning snort, and all three deer went bounding for cover, our wounded yearling keeping up with no difficulty. He even took the lead for the first few jumps.

That all happened a long time ago, but I still hold an abiding dislike for eagles.

18

Some Moose Are Soreheads

A few days before our camping trip on the Stuart ended, we put up a canvas tarp for a lean-to on the riverbank only a few yards from a snug hunting cabin that belonged to Charlie Davidson, a friend of ours and one of the best woodsmen and hunters I have ever known.

We'd have camped inside the cabin but for one reason. Pack rats had found a way to get into the place, and it was overrun with them. John and I agreed we'd have more peace and comfort, and less disturbed sleep, in the lean-to tent outside. If the weather turned bad, we could always move in with the rats.

Shortly after dark the second night we camped there, we were awakened by a sudden loud commotion in the willows hardly more than ten yards from our tent. Something big and heavy was crashing through the brush, and it seemed to be coming straight for us.

We were wide awake, on our feet, and out of the lean-to quicker than you can say it, and the noise stopped.

We stood for maybe a minute, staring into the darkness, trying to see what was out there in the deep shadows of the brush. Nothing stirred, no whisper of sound broke the stillness of the windless night. Yet we knew that in those shadows something was waiting, motionless as we were, something wild and dangerous and certainly big enough, from the sound of its crashing approach, to be deadly if it came on. What was it?

When we got the answer, it fairly lifted us out of our tracks. Suddenly, without so much as the sound of breathing to forewarn us, the willows shook to a hollow coughlike bellow so close it seemed to explode in our faces.

"That's a bear," John cried. He had his rifle ready, and he took a couple of quick steps to one side in the hope of getting a look at what had bellowed.

But I knew he was wrong in his identification. I had heard the grunting and bawling of bull moose enough times to be sure that this was not a bear.

Whatever it was, it was literally in our laps. But it came no closer. It bellowed again and then moved slowly toward the river, keeping to the dense cover and grunting every few steps. I had never heard any grunts that sounded crosser.

"It's a bear," John said again, and started to pad cautiously toward it, ready for a shot if it broke out of the willows.

"No, John, it's a bull moose," I told him. "And don't go any nearer. When they're in the mood that one's in, they're as treacherous as any bear. If he comes, he'll be out of the brush and on top of you before you can shoot."

"I still think it's a bear," John muttered.

He took two or three more cautious steps and stopped. Our night visitor had stopped too, still hidden in the shadows of the thicket. It was standing its ground there, probably waiting for us to make the next move.

Then it grunted again, that same hoarse bawling noise, closer to John than he had expected, and he took the hint. He came back far faster than he had sneaked after it.

"Let's get into the cabin," he urged. "Moose or bear, that thing is as mean as a sore tooth!"

We ran for the cabin door, and then there was a ludicrous bit of interference. In the dim light of the star-filled night I saw a skunk running across the little clearing, headed for the same destination we were.

I've had enough unhappy encounters with skunks that I'd walk a mile to avoid one, but that was no time to let my dread rule me. Whatever the skunk might do, it was far less to be feared than the big beast in the willows. I didn't even break stride.

We and the skunk arrived at the cabin porch together. He dived under it, we burst into the cabin and slammed and barred the door behind us.

"Did you see that skunk?" John asked.

"See it?" I cried. "I almost fell over it."

"I thought you were afraid of 'em," he teased.

"I am," I acknowledged, "but I'm a lot more afraid of a bull moose on the warpath."

"That's no moose," he contradicted me again.

I knew better, but I couldn't convince him. I know of no other animal in the woods that has a vocabulary as varied and expressive as that of the moose. A cow coaxes her calf along with soft grunts. Inviting a bull to come to her in mating time, she sounds much like a domestic cow mooing through her nose, and the bull talks back with low guttural snorts, almost like those of an aroused stallion under like circumstances. But when a rival challenges him or he gets his dander up for whatever reason, he warns the world with a roaring, chopping-on-a-hollow-log bellow, half bawl and half grunt, that's enough to make any man's hair stand on end. That was what John and I had heard.

With us out of sight, scent, and hearing inside the cabin, the moose quieted down, and in a little while John and I turned in, in one of the bunks. We slept well enough in spite of the pack rats, but when we awoke at daylight, John took his rifle and started down along the river, determined to drive off whatever had disturbed us if it was still hanging around and kill it if it proved to be a bear.

I finally proved my point. A quarter mile down the Stuart a big broad-antlered bull moose stepped out of the brush ahead of him. Whatever had aroused its anger the night before was forgotten now. It stopped at the river's edge, looked back at John, waded in, and swam to the far bank, and trotted swiftly into the willows. We saw no more of it.

"It's a good thing for that loudmouth that moose season isn't open yet," John told me when he got back to camp. "There was a winter's eating in him, and I'd have liked nothing better than to pay him for the scare he gave us last night."

How real had our danger been? Real enough.

The late Eric Collier, who lived for years in the British Columbia mountains at Meldrum Lake about one hundred and fifty miles south of us, close enough to make him almost a neighbor as wilderness neighbors go, once complained in a magazine article that he was sick of moose. They drove him off the trail on his trapline, he grumbled, chased him over his own garden fence, kept him from the outhouse, and even barged in on him when he sat down on a block of wood at the back door to hatch a story. Collier made his living as a professional writer.

In spite of the fact that I had depended on moose meat, fresh and canned, for our winter food supply those years while the children and I lived on the homestead, and it had meant the difference between eating well and going hungry (and although I have always enjoyed hunting moose, trying to outwit the big animals and get the best of them), there have been many times when I shared Eric Collier's feelings toward them. When they decide to make a nuisance of themselves they do a thorough job of it.

As for being dangerous, there is no animal in the woods more short-tempered and unpredictable than the bull moose in the time of rut, as the mating season is known. He stays mad at the world for days on end then, his anger constantly rekindled and fueled by the threat or actual presence of rival bulls.

I've known domestic bulls on cattle ranches and farms that were as dangerous to go near as a powder keg, and the same is true of bull moose under the right circumstances. They are supposed to be afraid of man and avoid him if they can, but once their temper flares they fear him no more than they fear another moose. I have known more than one case where a bull that had just won a fight with a rival turned on an approaching hunter with the same blind fury he had vented on the moose he had defeated.

Above all, they are unpredictable. Even in summer, months before the rut begins, a bull may flee from the sight or scent of humans one day but a day later stand his ground and even charge an approaching man headlong for no better reason than that he is feeling out of sorts. And now and then a cow will do the same thing, especially if she thinks her calf is being threatened.

I recall one incident in which Charlie Davidson, a neighbor of ours on the Stuart, encountered a cow and calf standing in the middle of the road on a cold winter day.

Charlie was on the way home from Vanderhoof with his car loaded with supplies, and had his wife and children along. The moose couldn't walk off the road because of the high banks piled up on either side by snowplows, and she refused flatly to get out of the way.

Charlie drove as close to her as he dared, blasted the car horn, climbed out and yelled, and finally threw his cap at her. She pounded it into the snow with her front feet. Next, he got a can of corn out of the food box and threw it. It belted her in the head, and that got action but not the kind he expected. She came for him headlong, and he scrambled back into the car and slammed the door behind him. The moose gave a few yards of ground, then stopped again and wouldn't budge.

It took the Davidsons exactly three hours to make a half mile, with Charlie alternately bombarding the cow with cans of food, then retreating to the safety of the car in the face of her angry rushes. They finally came to the place where the road divided, one fork leading to their place. They turned off on that fork, the moose walked ahead on the other one, and that ended the confrontation.

As for a wounded moose, it is fully as much to be shunned as a wounded bear.

We never did even the score with the bull that had threatened us that night at the Davidson cabin, but a few days later John had an encounter with another bull, equally hair-raising, and this time he emerged the winner. It was one of those occasions when the moose had won an argument with another of his own kind and turned on a man minutes later in blind rage, determined to drive off any living thing that trespassed near him.

The moose season opened three days before our camping trip was due to end. Both John and I had always enjoyed hunting, although I shrank from the actual shooting. In addition, I had hunted to feed my family much of my life, and he and I are fond of wild meat. We wanted a freezer full of moose for winter, so the morning the season opened we started looking for a bull of eating size.

In the ten or eleven days we had then been out, we had seen thirty-six moose—bulls, cows, and calves—all of them along the river. Some were feeding on lilies and weeds, others swimming across, a few standing quietly on the bank where the wind kept the worst of the flies away. But now that hunting was legal, there was not a bull moose to be found.

"John, I know where we can get a moose," I told my husband the last morning of our stay in camp.

"Where?"

"Down the river below Chief Louie Billie's cabin. Across from my old place. There are two small lakes back in there, with a meadow between. I don't think I ever went there at this time of year without seeing moose."

"Long way to pack the meat out," John objected.

I nodded agreement. "But that's better than having none to pack out," I argued. "On top of that, I'd like to show you those old hunting grounds of mine. I used to go there when I wanted to make sure the kids and I wouldn't go through a winter hungry."

"It's worth a try," John agreed. Then he added with a twinkle in his eyes, "If we kill a moose, you can carry out the four quarters and I'll take the horns. That's the way your Indian neighbors used to do it."

"I didn't marry one of my Indian neighbors," I retorted tartly.

We headed downriver to the location I had in mind, beached our boat, and started for the two small lakes. My predictions were borne out even sooner than I expected. When we came in sight of the first lake, creeping through the willows, a tall, long-legged bull with a splendid rack was crossing a narrow point of marsh on the far shore. He had his nose down to the ground, apparently following the track of a cow. It was coming to be that time of year.

For a man who enjoyed hunting as much as John did, he was carrying a very inferior rifle. It was an old Winchester .30/06, with a bad barrel that was as likely to send a bullet keyholing wide of the mark as on a true course.

Too, this moose was pretty far away for iron sights, maybe one hundred and fifty yards, and I wasn't surprised when John's first shot kicked up mud and water just ahead of its front feet. The bull's head came up, but he hadn't located the shot. He turned to look into the brush behind him, and John tried again. Again I saw mud fly, this time under the bull's belly. He still didn't know where the noise was coming from, but two shots in quick succession were all the hint he needed. Wherever the danger might be, the neighborhood had turned unhealthy. He hit for the brush at the long-strided, swinging trot of his kind, with water splashing in every direction, and John's third shot did no more good than the first two.

For a minute I was strongly tempted to make a pointed remark about the old rifle, along I-told-you-so lines, but I thought better of it and contented myself with a mild, "Too bad, but we'll likely find another one."

"I'm going to find another rifle, too," John growled. "You'd have to be inside a barn to hit the end of it with this one."

Sometimes, the less a wife says, the more likely she is to get her way, I reflected to myself. I had been urging a new rifle on John for a long time.

We turned down along the headwaters of Bear Creek, keeping to the top of ridges where we could look down on willow flats and small boggy openings, walking slowly and silently, knowing that the ears of a moose are far more likely to warn him of danger than his eyes. His nose has to be taken into account, too, for there are few animals in the woods with keener scent. But the wind was right that morning, and we had no worry on that score.

We had traveled less than a mile when we came to a torn and trampled place where two bull moose had been fighting.

"Early for this," I whispered to John. "Not quite time for the rut yet."

"Maybe it's early, but these two have been at it in earnest," he whispered back.

There was no doubt on that score. Brush and small trees had been broken down, the ground gouged and scarred, and there were patches of moose hair as big as a man's hand scattered around. The fight had been a battle royal.

It had happened less than an hour before, too. The ground was freshly torn and, surest sign of all, the rank smell of moose still hung over the place.

"Do you smell them?" I asked.

John nodded and held up a warning finger. "They're not far off," he whispered. "I think we're going to kill our moose."

We started down the slope of a low hill, trying to move without rattling leaves or breaking twigs. Then suddenly the thick brush below us exploded with a crash, and a bull broke out of a thicket, running full tilt straight at us.

It turned out that he had a cow in the brush with him. Almost certainly he had just emerged the victor in the battle at the top of the hill. Probably he had heard us coming and mistaken us for his rival returning to renew the argument. If he realized his mistake now that he was in the open and could see us clearly, he was in too ugly a frame of mind to care.

I have lived with moose most of my life, and when a bull is thoroughly aroused, especially in courting time, I rate him as dangerous as any animal in the woods.

This one was coming with head lowered, ears laid back, eyes wild, the coarse hair on his shoulders all standing the wrong way. Every couple of steps he let out the same kind of hollow, coughing grunts that we had heard a few nights before in front of our lean-to.

John was standing a few feet off to one side of me, his rifle up, waiting for a clear shot. I was holding my breath, remembering the earlier performance of that old gun. If he missed this time, there wasn't much question what would happen, for the bull was beside itself with anger, and only one thing could stop it.

It all happened in far less time than I can tell it, but almost at the last minute, I heard a low coaxing grunt in the brush the bull had left, and out of the tail of my eye I caught a glimpse of a cow standing there, switching her ridiculous stub of a tail back and forth.

Then John's rifle cracked and the bull went up on its hind legs like a rearing stallion, hung there a second or two almost as upright as a human, toppled backward, and fell heavily. He hardly kicked after he went down, and in the thickets below I saw the cow running like a streak of lightning.

The first thing John said, with a crooked smile, was, "Well, we've got our winter's meat supply."

"Are you ready now to admit what we heard in the brush the other night?" I asked when the excitement had quieted down.

"The same thing we heard just now," John admitted with a grin.

Packing the four quarters of that heavy-bodied bull out to the road was no easy chore, but we did it and drove home to Prince George delighted with the ending of our camping trip.

I no longer had to hunt moose for food. I could hunt them for fun now. But I have always liked wild meat better than any other kind, and the food was still very welcome.

19

The Bears I Have Met

A few years after John and I were married, we bought a sawmill near Prince George and settled down to running a logging and sawmill operation. It was routine work, almost too lacking in excitement to suit either of us, except for one thing. The bears of the neighborhood elected to save us from boredom, and they did a thorough and tireless job of it, as bears are likely to do. Once they have raided a place and found it to their liking, they rarely stay away for long. Certainly that was the case this time.

We had bears at our garbage dump, bears prowling around the buildings, bears at the door at night. They were all blacks and we had little fear of them, but they were a nuisance, and there was one other complicating factor—a small fox terrier named Jeep.

I had acquired him about a year before, as a small pup. He was not big enough to deal with the bears and never would be, but that was something he himself was totally unaware of. He hated the sight and smell of them and took on the self-appointed task of camp guard, determined to run them off as fast as they showed up.

Jeep had more grit than sense, which is a common trait of his breed, and I was sure that sooner or later a bear was going to stand up to him and I'd have to get a new dog. It got so that every time I heard him barking I'd run out to give him a hand or call him off.

We put up with the bears for weeks, but finally the inevitable happened. A big boar grew bolder than the rest, ripped the screens off the meat house one night, climbed in, and helped himself. He didn't seem to like fresh beef, but he cleaned up our bacon, summer sausage, and pork, either eating it on the spot or carrying it off.

John and I agreed he'd have to be disposed of without any delay. After that one successful break-in, he'd be back night after night, and the sooner we killed him the better.

We cut a four-inch opening in the cook-house door overlooking the scene of his raid, a peephole just big enough to poke a gun barrel through. We'd keep watch for him out of the cook-house window. He didn't keep us waiting. He came in shortly after dark the first night, walked straight to the window behind which we were posted, as if aware we were there, stood up with his big muddy paws on the glass, and stared in.

We had ducked back into a corner, and I'm not really afraid of bears, as I said, but I'll admit it made my scalp prickle to look that one in the face only six or eight feet away, with nothing but a pane of glass between us. John could have killed him easily but didn't want to break the window, so he waited until the bear dropped down and started for the meat house.

He poked his .30/06, a Winchester Model 54, out of the peephole. The bear was only a step or two away from the muzzle. The shot hit him in the ribs, and he bawled and made a rush between the cook house and meat house. The opening wasn't more than two feet wide, and there was more bear than that. He slammed into the side of the cook house so hard that every dish on the shelves rattled, but he squeezed through and ran for the brush.

John ran out after him, but I wanted no part of chasing a wounded bear in the black of night, so I stood at the window and tried to help by pointing a flashlight. When John heard him break brush beyond the clearing, he gave up and came back.

As soon as daylight came we went out and let Jeep take the blood trail. We jumped the bear half a mile from camp, and John stopped him with a hip shot. He was still full of fight, snarling and thrashing around, and the fox terrier came within a hair of getting himself converted into dogburger before John wound things up with a 180-grain softpoint in the side of the bear's head.

Looking back, it seems to me that I have been pestered by trouble-hunting bears most of my grown-up life.

The first one was the short-tempered old female that came for me when I met her and her three cubs on the way back to my homestead on the Stuart from a trip to a neighbor's house for mail. I outran her, but I suppose only for the reason that she decided she didn't want to clobber me after all. I'm sure no person could get away from a bear that was really determined to attack. They may look clumsy, but they can cover ground at an astonishing rate, especially for a short distance. A horse needs a good start to stay ahead of one, particularly on rough ground.

The next one I'll never forget was the sow with the two cubs that caught and killed the little fawn the day John and I were on a hike along the Fraser just out of Prince George, before we were married. That was a horrid thing to see, and the memory will stay with me as long as I live.

I'll say one thing in defense of bears, however. Even that time the sow made a swift and merciful kill. She wasted no time, and there was none of the tearing and torment that characterizes an attack by wolves.

After we killed the one that was raiding the meat house, we had no more bear problems that we couldn't put up with for two or three years. Then, after we had moved to a ranch on the Stuart River, another came along that gave us enough trouble to get himself shot.

In April, shortly after our lambs and calves arrived, we began losing them to a bear. We did everything we could think of, keeping watch of the stock daytimes, penning it near the barn at night in the belief the killer would not come close to the buildings. But he was bold and persistent, and we continued to find dead sheep almost every morning.

Finally we decided to go looking for him. Because it was still early in the spring, it seemed likely he'd be hanging around in the vicinity of his winter den. Maybe we could find that. We still had Jeep and he was as dedicated to bear fights as ever, so we took him along.

It was he that made the find. We heard him barking in a thick stand of young aspen, and when we got there he was fussing and fuming around a big hole under a stump. There were claw marks on all the nearby trees. We had discovered a bear den, all right, but whether it was the right bear or whether the owner was in it remained to be seen. Jeep seemed very sure on the latter score, however.

If the bear was home, he paid no attention to the racket our pint-sized dog was making, nor did John get any response when he poked into the den with a long pole. But when he made his next move, things started happening.

John peeled off an old shirt he was wearing, wrapped it around the end of the pole, set it afire, and rammed it down into the hole. There was a brief pause, then a loud sneeze followed by a throaty grunt, more sneezing, and a gruff cough. At that point the pole started to shake, and I shoved John's .30/06 into his hands. A split second later the head of a very upset bear emerged from beneath the stump. John didn't let him come any farther. He slapped his shot between the eyes at six feet. It turned out that we killed the right bear, too. We lost no more sheep.

The bear encounter that I rate the most unusual I ever had was one that happened to John and me the year we prospected for gold in the Omineca River country north of Germansen Landing. That was a thoroughly happy summer, and I'll tell of it in a chapter that follows.

As for the bears, John and I were hiking along a nameless creek one day in June. We had stopped at the top of a ridge in the foothills of the Wolverine Mountains when suddenly brush started to break down the slope to our left.

The sound wasn't right for moose, deer, or caribou. Mixed with the crashing of brush, we could hear hard thudding noises, as if two men were pummeling each other with boxing gloves. Plainly a fight of some kind was going on, but there was no growling or grunting, nothing to hint at the identity of the fighters.

We started to sneak closer, taking one careful step after another, moving brush aside with our hands to avoid rustling leaves and twigs. And suddenly the explanation of what was taking place flashed through my mind, and I knew what we were stalking, or at least I thought I did. This was June, the mating season for black bears. We were listening to two males settling an argument for possession of a lady friend.

I touched John on the shoulder, and when he looked around at me I formed the word "Bears!" soundlessly with my lips.

The light wind flowing down off the snow peaks of the Wolverines was in our favor. John was carrying a .30/06 Winchester, so we knew we could protect ourselves, and we crept close enough for a ringside seat at the strangest brawl we have ever watched.

Two big black bears were standing face to face in a half-open space in a stand of scrub aspen, sparring like a pair of clumsy boxers. But the method of punching was different.

First one bear and then the other would open his big, hairy

arms wide apart as if readying for an embrace. Then he'd lunge in and land a swinging pile-driver blow.

Most of the blows struck on the head and shoulders and didn't seem to do a great deal of damage. But now and then one bear or the other got walloped in the belly, and that must have hurt, for as often as it happened there'd be a sharp grunt of pain.

A couple of times we saw one bear lock a forearm around a tree, as if to brace himself, and deliver a blow that actually lifted his opponent off his feet and knocked him to the ground.

The battle was coming to a climax now, and there was much snarling and whining that we had not heard earlier, but still John and I, crouched in a thicket only a few yards away, could see little evidence of serious damage. One was bleeding around the mouth and face, but that was the only sign they were using teeth or claws.

Once they backed away from each other and stood looking downwind. John winked at me and we both grinned, sure that somewhere in the brush in that direction the cause of the fight was watching and waiting.

Then they rushed each other once more and went into a clinch, growling and blowing, each making a determined effort for the first time to use his teeth. They bit savagely at one another's neck and shoulders, and then one lunged for a front foot of his opponent. It was a lightning-swift grab, square on target. He caught the forepaw between his jaws, and we saw him crunch down.

The victim let out a scream of pain that was almost human, hooked the claws of his free foot in the fur at the top of the other bear's head, and tried frantically to pull free. But the teeth were locked in his paw like the spiked jaws of a steel trap. He screamed again, and clawed and bit, but could not free himself, and it was plain that he had lost the fight. Once he got loose, that forepaw would be out of action, and he'd stand little chance. My guess was that he'd run off as soon as he could.

The deadlock lasted for close to a minute, and the bawls of the victim were as blood-chilling as anything I have ever listened to. Then a fluke ended the battle. The wind shifted, and the female bear, hidden in the thick cover down the slope from us, caught scent of John and me.

We heard a warning snort from her, a sound much like that of a frightened horse, and the two males parted as if a lightning bolt had slammed into the ground between them. They had no idea what the danger was or where it lay, but they didn't wait to find out.

The unhurt one ran downhill toward the sow, the other limped around a jumble of rocks on three feet and went quickly out of sight. Three or four minutes later the victorious boar and the female, an unusually big sow, walked into an opening one hundred and fifty yards away, stopped briefly and looked back, then vanished in the brush at a dead run.

John and I had watched a duel that is a common happening everywhere in bear country. Many boars, both blacks and grizzlies, taken by hunters and trappers are terribly scarred around the face and head from just such battles, fought for the same reason. But it's rare for humans to witness an encounter of that kind.

It's not uncommon for a man to come across two bull moose contending for a cow in no-quarter battle, but in a lifetime in bear country, only a few times have I known anyone to watch a fight between male bears. I suppose the explanation lies in part in their natural wariness and secretive ways, in part because the greater share of their prowling, and also of their courting and fighting, is done in the black of night.

I myself had seen bears fight on two or three other occasions but always down on all four, snapping and slashing at each other like angry dogs. The thing that was so very different about these two, and that made their fight of such unusual interest, was the fact that they elected to slug it out erect on their hind legs, for all the world like human boxers. I still have no theory to explain why they did it, and I have never heard of another bout like it.

Another time, on a creek running into the Stuart, John and I sat and watched a small black bear catching salmon by a method all his own.

He was fishing in shallow water and slapping the fish out on the bank with a scoop of his paw. He'd wait until he saw one he wanted, in a place where the creek ran over a gravel shoal, make a swipe, and the salmon would land on the bank, eight or ten feet away. He'd wade ashore, eat what he wanted, and go back for another.

That was the only bear we had ever seen catch fish that way. Many times we had seen pictures in magazines of bears doing that, and we had always ridiculed the artist for not knowing what he was doing, for every bear we had ever watched, black or grizzly, caught his salmon by pinning them down in the water with jaws or forepaws, grabbing the fish by the back, and usually breaking its spine with one savage shake, then carrying it to the bank in his teeth.

This little black oddball was an exception to what we had always thought was a universal rule, but his way of doing it worked as well as the standard procedure.

The bear that I remember as well as any, and with good cause, was a big male that came around the last sawmill we operated.

Nuisance blacks were plentiful at that location, and we had to kill several, but this one was in a class by himself. He was smart enough to limit his visits to the late hours of night after we had turned in, when everything was quiet, and he was a real expert at tearing things apart. He broke into the meat house, figured out a way to get at our hens, and finally tore the top off our rabbit pen, reached in, and helped himself. Fed up with his raids, we baited him with fresh meat, strung tin cans on a wire for an alarm, and rigged a spotlight to illuminate the scene for shooting.

It was close to daylight when we heard the cans rattle. John jumped up and shoved a couple of shells into the .30/06, thinking that was all he'd need, and I dived for the spotlight. But before I could switch it on, he stopped me. "There's light enough to shoot by," he said. "The spotlight might scare him off."

We had four other people in our quarters—a high-strung, excitable woman who helped me, and three hired hands, including a Norwegian by the name of Oscar Norden. Oscar and the woman shared a very healthy fear of bears.

Before John could get the door open, the hired girl was rushing around, bumping into things, and muttering cusswords in a steady stream. She must have rattled John, for he put his shot too far back. The bear went down, growling and flailing around only a few feet from the door. Then everything got quiet, and John stepped out to check, with the hired men right at his heels. It didn't occur to me that I should turn on the spotlight at that point, and the four of them went tiptoeing cautiously toward the meat house. All of a sudden brush cracked behind them, the bear cut loose with a blood-chilling growl, and the four bear hunters came for the house in a hurry. One of the hired hands tripped and fell and lost a shoe, but it didn't slow him much, for they all arrived at the porch at the same time. John took time then to fire another shot but missed in the deep shadows, and four men came through the door together. The bear was right at their heels, too. Somebody knocked a mop down, the handle blocked the door so it couldn't be latched, and pandemonium broke loose inside the house.

John's gun was empty, and he yelled for more shells. The hired girl grabbed the box but then climbed up on the kitchen sink and forgot she had them. She perched there, cussing at the top of her voice. We still had the little fox terrier, and he was still too small to take a hand in an affair of that kind but didn't know it. He was barking furiously and I was hanging onto him, and Oscar Norden was hopping around the room, yelling, "Where's that dammit ax? Yust let me get the ax!" When things quieted down a little, we could hear the bear growling and pawing his way along the side of the house as if he were trying to find a way to get in. He never did discover the unlatched door.

In the end we got things sorted out, fastened the door, and found the box of shells for John. He reloaded, and I remembered to switch on the spotlight. When John stepped around the corner of the house, the bear was only ten feet away. It had time to rear up and let go one defiant bawl, and then John finished it with a shot in the head. It fell about one long step away from him.

Bears? You can have 'em. They are born troublemakers, and I made up my mind many years ago that if as long as I live I ever tangle with one again, it will be the bear's doing, not mine.

20

The Lure of Gold

In December of 1943, John's airline transferred him from Prince George to Port Hardy, at the north end of Vancouver Island, and we lived there or in Vancouver until after the end of World War II.

John enjoyed it, but I can't say that I did. The fishing was very good, and he caught big salmon, ling, rock cod, flounder, and sole galore. We picked up seashells along the beach, dug clams at low tide, and hunted crabs. We built a small cabin boat, powered with a fifteen-horsepower inboard engine, and took some pleasant gypsy trips along the sheltered coast of Vancouver Island and the adjoining mainland.

It was fun but for some reason not quite satisfying for me. I never came to like the ocean. Maybe it was too big and empty for someone who had lived all her life in the mountains. I grew more and more hungry for the snow peaks, the lush valleys, the creeks and rivers of my girlhood. I had my roots down there.

About a year after the war ended, Pan American closed the facility at Port Hardy and offered John a job at Whitehorse, in Yukon Territory just north of the British Columbia border. But neither he nor I wanted to move there. We talked it over and agreed he'd leave the airline, and we would go into something for ourselves, maybe a sawmill or a ranch somewhere along the Stuart River, in my old stamping grounds.

But first, we decided, we'd have a summer to ourselves, of the kind we both liked best, a summer of wilderness living. We were both sick to death of towns and cities and crowds. We'd go north and pan for gold in the wild mountain country around the Omineca River. John had prospected there before and knew what we'd find, but it would all be new to me.

I had cherished a dream of gold prospecting for many years, but only once had I been in gold country. That was the time I worked in the camp of Germansen Landing, and there was never a spare hour in those months to go hiking off and search for gold.

Now the thoughts of a summer in the bush—the bird songs, the music of running water, the sight of the stars coming out at dusk, the northern lights dancing their eerie heel and toe across the velvet of the midnight sky—with the knowledge that we had it all to ourselves, I could hardly wait to get started.

"Are you sure it's the kind of vacation you want?" John asked me more than once.

"It'll be the best vacation two people ever had," I told him.

When we announced our plans to my daughters, Olive and Vala, who were living then in Edmonton, we drew a torrent of protest. We must be out of our minds, they cried, to go off into the mountains, miles from the nearest settlement, and spend months where we could not hope to see another human. What would happen if one of us fell ill? What about accidents? There were many other what-will-you-do-if-this-or-that-should-happen questions, but none of them swayed John or me. We knew what we wanted, and our minds were made up.

One question the girls did not raise, probably because they didn't think of it, was the likelihood that we might encounter a quarrelsome grizzly or two. It's a risk that anyone must take who ventures into grizzly country, for whatever the nature lovers and wild-animal apologists may say to the contrary, the humpbacked bear is short-tempered and deadly dangerous at close quarters. As things turned out, grizzlies would prove the most serious threat we would face that summer.

We put our outfit together with care, knowing that we would be away from settlements, even from trading posts, the entire time. But, at the same time, we kept our supplies and equipment as light as was practical since there'd be backpacking involved in reaching many of the places where we wanted to go.

John said we'd find cabins scattered through the country, built by prospectors and trappers. Some had been there many years and would be tumbledown, and we'd have to fix them up. Others would be fairly new, left unlocked by their owners for the summer. We'd be welcome to use any we found.

We'd pick two or three of those cabins that we could reach by boat, establish our base camps there and cache our food supplies and equipment, and hike out on short trips to the creeks we wanted to pan, carrying only the things we needed.

We limited our supplies to bacon and salt pork, beans and rice, dried eggs and dried vegetables, tea, coffee, and as much flour as we thought we could carry. For the rest, we'd live off the land. We knew there would be trout in every creek and river, lake trout and grayling in the lakes. British Columbia game regulations also allowed a prospector to kill game if he needed it for food.

John had long since acquired a new barrel for his Winchester .30/06. It shot as straight as a die, and I'd carry a .30-30 or a .22. We had not the slightest misgivings about going hungry in a place so rich in fish and game.

We'd start from Summit Lake, about forty miles north of Prince George. In May, as soon as the ice was out of the lakes and rivers, we hired a truck to take us and our outfit that far.

We had two boats, one a narrow thirty-six-footer, the other a small riverboat eighteen feet long, with outboards for each of them. The bigger boat was powered with a fourteen-horsepower motor, the smaller one with a three-horse. When we were hitting out on a long trip, we could load the eighteen-footer inside the big one, along with our outfit, and avoid the necessity of towing.

At Summit Lake we loaded up and headed down the Crooked River that would take us to McLeod Lake, another sixty or seventy miles north.

The Crooked is a bucky little stream, with enough sharp bends to justify its name, and at that time of year it was bank full and running like an express train. Our boat was carrying a heavy load, and in spite of all John could do, with the outboard running fast enough to give us steerage way, time after time as we rounded a hairpin bend, the boat would smash its nose into the bank, swing broadside in the current, and threaten to capsize. But my husband was a good riverman, and water that left me shaking with fright didn't worry him in the least.

At the Hudson's Bay Company post and Indian reserve at the north end of McLeod Lake, we left settlements and people behind. If we saw another human apart from each other the rest of the summer, it would be a roving family of Indians or other prospectors like ourselves. We were going it alone from here on, and we knew there were challenges ahead, but we both welcomed them.

From the north end of McLeod we ran the short stretch of the Pack to where it joins the Parsnip, then down the Parsnip to the Finlay near Finlay Forks, and followed the Finlay upstream toward the Wolverine Mountains, through a wide and lovely valley.

"This will be farmland someday," I told John.

"Glad we're seeing it first," he grunted. "I like the looks of moose better than cows."

All the way after we left McLeod Lake, in the mud along the

shores of the rivers and creeks we were traveling, we saw bear sign and tracks too big to have been left by blacks.

They worried me. I have never been really afraid of black bears, in spite of the many encounters and arguments I have had with them, but the grizzly is another story. If the wilderness has a king, the title belongs to him. He fears nothing that walks the woods, save man, and his fear of man is likely to be easily overcome.

Like all bears, he is totally unpredictable, a bumbling, harmless-looking clown-in-fur one minute, a maniacal bundle of red-eyed fury the next. His temper is as short as it is terrible, and I have always believed that the bear himself does not know when he will fly into a rage or what will light the quick fuse of his anger. One thing I do know—from all the grizzly stories I have heard and read, as well as from my own limited experience with them and that of woodsmen with whom I have been acquainted—enraged, the grizzly will attack anything on earth, man included. The only safe rule where he is concerned is to avoid him if you can.

But now we were going to summer in an area of mountains where that might prove impossible, and the more bear tracks we saw, the less I liked it. Some of those tracks showed claw marks longer than John's fingers, and they sent chills up my spine. But when I voiced my worries, John laughed at me. "Likely we won't see a bear all summer," he predicted.

He could hardly have been more wrong. Before the trip ended, we saw close to a dozen grizzlies and were plagued by as many more that we didn't see. They demolished our camps, raided our food caches, stole our dried fish, left us to go hungry at the end of a long hike time after time, and raised cain in general, of the kind that only a trouble-hunting bear can dream up. You have to see a cabin one has torn apart to realize what damage they are capable of.

Luckily, of all the grizzlies we encountered, only two were looking for a fight. But those two were more than enough.

We traveled fast. Three days from Summit Lake brought us to an old cabin on the bank of the Omineca. It was small and tumble-down, and a corner of the roof had fallen in. But we cut poles for new rafters, patched it up, named it Cabin No. 1, and moved in. We'd cache part of our supplies here to avoid taking them on up the river.

This was primitive country, wild, untouched, beautiful. The Omineca crawled with trout. Almost any time, a half hour of fishing would get us all we could eat in a day. The river was clear and ice-cold, with long rock-broken stretches and deep runs between, and the trout were firm and delicious. For days on end we lived on fried trout and fresh bread that I baked in a small camp-stove oven.

I have eaten elaborate meals in some of the best restaurants in Vancouver and the other cities of western Canada, and I'll stack against the greatest of them trout from a cold mountain river, so fresh-caught that they curl when you drop them into the hot grease, served up with hot bread from a rusty little oven. Of course, the setting has to be right. There must be the smells of wood smoke and pine needles and sun-warmed earth drifting in through the open door of a low-roofed cabin as you eat, and snow peaks in the far distance are a help.

We had been at Cabin No. 1 a few days when John went hunting one morning and left me by myself. I tidied up the camp, and once the chores were finished I took the water bucket off its stand behind the door and started for the spring where we got our drinking water. It bubbled out from beneath an overhanging shelf of rock at the foot of a slope grown rank with vetch and peavine, and the spot was pretty and restful enough to be worth visiting whether we needed water or not.

I had almost reached the spring, completely at peace with the world, reflecting how lucky I was to be so far away from the bustle and noise of town, traffic, hurrying crowds of people, even telephones. I stopped to take a deep breath and savor the clean fresh air and the mixed fragrance of pine and wildflowers distilled by the warm sun of early summer.

"This is the most wonderful life in the world," I whispered to myself. And then a movement above the shelving rock that sheltered the spring caught my eye. It was a small movement, noiseless and furtive, but something warned me that a large animal had made it, and for some reason the breath caught in my throat.

I forgot all about the beauty of the morning, the clean air, and the good smells. I stood stock-still, searching the brush where I had seen the movement, trying to tell myself that it might have been John, watching a grouse or rabbit, but not able to believe it.

Some inner sense seemed to warn me there was danger there by the spring, and I started to tremble—strange behavior for a grown woman who had lived most of her life in the mountains, as I had.

I stayed motionless, letting my eyes quest that thick green slope, and suddenly I saw it.

A puff of wind stirred a thicket, and through an opening among the leaves the sun struck on the head and foreleg of a huge bear. I had a clear view for only a second or two, but in that flash of time I saw enough to know that I was looking at a very big grizzly, and he was looking at me. I glimpsed the long brown hair on the leg, the telltale dished face, and half the head and one ear. From that brief look I would know that bear from all the other grizzlies in British Columbia if we met again. The ear and a small area of fur around it were snow-white.

It's not unusual to encounter a bear with a patch of white on the throat, and I have seen them with one partly white paw, but this was the first one I had ever seen with white around the face or head.

I dropped my bucket, whirled, and ran for the cabin with fright lending wings to my feet. I've been told many times that to run from a wild animal is to invite pursuit and even attack, but that was no time to think of the rules of correct behavior. I didn't even remember them. I was afraid of grizzlies, and this one, staring at me no more than a hundred feet away, had pushed me to the verge of panic.

I grabbed my .30-30 off the cabin wall and stepped back outside. From the direction of the spring, I heard a loud thump, and then my bucket went clattering through the brush where I had dropped it. When the affair was over with, I found that he had sent it flying with a swat that half crumpled it. It was a man thing, and I suppose he didn't like the way it smelled.

I ran around the corner of the cabin for a better look. My hands were shaking, and I remember thinking that that was no way to behave if I expected to kill the grizzly. I'd better steady down and make my first shot count.

I didn't get that first shot, and maybe it was just as well. My .30-30 was on the light side for such a bear, and if I had wounded him and failed to kill, I'd almost surely have been in deadly danger.

As I rounded the corner of the cabin, I caught one more glimpse of him. His broad, burly rump was vanishing in a thick tangle of red osier halfway down the slope to the spring. I saw just enough to know that this was the biggest bear I had ever laid eyes on. He was gone before I could shoot.

I waited two or three hours before I ventured after my bucket. Then I took the rifle along, naturally. The bear had smashed the water pail out of shape with one blow. But I saw or heard no more of him, and I straightened it out as best I could and went on to the spring.

When John got back to the cabin that afternoon, we went together to look for the grizzly's tracks. Set crosswise in one of them, my size-four shoe didn't quite span it.

"That's quite a bear," John acknowledged. "I wouldn't want him to get his arms around you."

"I don't want to see him again," I retorted. "If this is where he hangs out, I'll be glad to get away."

We gave the grizzly the name White-Ear, not dreaming then where and how his trail and ours would continue to cross throughout the summer.

There was something uncanny about those meetings. It seemed that no matter in which direction we went, he was there ahead of us or arrived shortly after we did. We did a lot of traveling that summer, and so did the white-eared bear. I suppose the explanation was that we had moved into his home range and were covering country that he had considered his long before we came along.

In any case, none of the encounters was friendly. White-Ear hated humans and had no fear of them at all. He was to prove a very dangerous neighbor.

At the end of a couple of weeks we left Cabin No. 1, took our smaller boat, and went fourteen miles farther up the Omineca to a lake that we named End Lake. There was one fairly long portage, and our boat was too heavy to carry. But we made skids for it by laying green aspen poles parallel on the ground, about a foot apart. The two of us could pull the boat on those poles as on a track, moving it ahead a length or two, then picking up the poles and relaying them in front of it again. Two people can make good time that way if they know how and if the portage is not too rough and steep.

John had said that we'd find another cabin at End Lake. We did, but that wasn't all we found. We started to carry our outfit up from the shore, and when we came in sight of the cabin, set in a small clearing, we stopped short, staring in astonishment.

The cabin was of small pine logs and not strongly built, old and small and tumbledown, much like No. 1. But that was not what surprised us. It was the way the little low-roofed structure was leaning at a crazy, tilted angle.

"What the hell has happened here?" John muttered.

"Could it have been an earthquake?" I suggested.

John shook his head. "It's hard to believe, but my guess is a bear," he said.

We walked on, staring at the funny lopsided way the whole cabin stood, and John plopped his foot in a pile of bear droppings.

"I thought so," he growled.

When we looked things over we found tracks, and claw and tooth marks on the door and log ends of the place—and to me the tracks looked alarmingly like those of White-Ear.

John and I talked it over that night and decided that while we'd never be sure, it could easily be the same bear. The grizzly is a traveler, and although we had covered fourteen miles by river and lake between the two cabins, it was entirely logical to think that both of them might lie within the territory this one prowled.

An old, hungry grizzly with bad teeth that killed an Indian hunter in northern British Columbia in January of 1970 left the area after he was disturbed at his kill, and traveled eight miles of airline distance in a single night. He was tracked and killed from a helicopter since British Columbia game authorities considered it too dangerous to go after him in heavy cover on foot.

"John, I'm afraid of that bear," I confessed.

"You'll be all right," he assured me. "But don't ever leave camp without a gun."

We put in a few days repairing the bear damage and fixing the place up, named it Cabin No. 3 since it was the last of a line of three that we planned to use during the summer, and moved in.

End Lake had a fantastic population of Dolly Varden, rainbow, and lake trout, and I seriously doubt that anyone had ever wet a line in it before that summer. It was virgin water, and the trout were as easily caught as sunfish in a millpond. We took them, mostly Dolly Vardens but now and then a lake trout or rainbow weighing up to twelve pounds, on any kind of lure we used. Once, when we were crossing the lake and had no fishhooks along, we improvised a hook with a safety pin and caught enough for supper in a few minutes. A small rag of red cloth tied on a hook was about as deadly on that lake as any spoon.

The summer moved along. July came and huckleberries started to ripen, and John and I went out one afternoon to pick enough for supper.

We had about half what we wanted when we heard brush break up the hillside a short distance away, and a medium-sized grizzly stepped into sight. It was also picking berries and hadn't seen us. John took a few quick steps to where his rifle was leaning against a tree, and the movement caught the bear's eye.

It went up on its hind feet, erect as a man, and stared our way for a lagging half minute, swinging its head from side to side and sniffing to get scent of us. Then it let go a hair-raising bawl, dropped to all fours, and ran.

I was drawing a long breath of relief when it came my turn to see movement. Something was smashing through thick brush behind John, coming for him at a dead run. It broke into the open, and I saw that it was a second bear, smaller than the first— just the right size to be quarrelsome because it didn't know any better.

"John! Behind you!" I screamed.

He whirled, brought his rifle to his shoulder, and fired, all in one motion. The heavy soft-nose slug from the .30/06 smashed into the bear's head between the eyes, and the animal piled up stone-dead, only thirty to forty yards away.

I saw John turn and stare up the hill, the way the first grizzly had run. "That was a mother and son team," he told me. "This one is about a yearling, and the old girl may decide to come back."

She didn't, but that ended our berry picking for that day.

We put in the next couple of weeks with grub, a tent, and the rest of our equipment in backpacks, panning.

Panning is the most primitive of all methods of gold mining. But in my opinion, it's also the most fun.

It's a single-handed operation. The miner scoops up a panful of sand, gravel, and water in a shallow basin and swirls it with a rotating motion, letting the contents slop over the rim. The mud is washed away, while the heavier gold, either the specks known as dust, or nuggets if the panner has exceptional luck, settles to the bottom. At the end only the gold is left. It's a slow process, and it takes many pans to yield an ounce of gold even in good pay dirt, but the excitement and suspense and promise of a rich find are always there.

There is some magic quality about gold beyond its monetary value. There has to be, or men would not have suffered the hardships they have, and risked their lives as willingly, in the quest for it—often a quest that failed. And nowhere is the tug of its lure stronger than on a sandbar in some remote wilderness river, when a solitary prospector scoops up a pan of dirt and gravel, washes it until the last grain of sand has been splashed out, and sees the bright glint of "color" in the bottom of his pan. He has found gold, and for all he knows, the riches of Midas may be buried in the sand beneath his feet, his for the panning. Gold fever hits him and hits him hard. It's a heady business, and John and I loved every minute of it.

The Indians of the area did not share our feelings, however. We encountered them on the streams several times as the summer went along. One came by one day when I was panning by myself. The idea of gold panning had always seemed to amuse them, and I decided I'd try to make a convert of this one.

He stood and watched silently while I washed a couple of pans of gravel. In the second one I had luck. A nugget a quarter the size of a pea lay in the bottom of the pan. I held it up and made my pitch.

"You get gold," I said, tapping the tiny nugget, "you trade um. Get tobacco, get flour, get sugar. Have good food. Wear good boots."

His face relaxed in something that hinted at a disdainful grin. "Hard work, get gold," he told me loftily. That ended the sermon.

We didn't strike it rich along the Omineca. In fact, we barely struck gold at all.

"There are better creeks than this," John promised me one night beside our campfire. "There's the Ingenika, the Osilinka, the Mesilinka and the Pelly, and a dozen more I know about that don't even have a name. The foothills between here and the Wolverines are laced with 'em. We'll find what we're looking for before the summer is over."

21

The Saga of White-Ear

In August, when the nights were turning frosty, we came back to End Lake from a couple of weeks of panning, making an all-day hike under heavy packs. John was carrying about one hundred pounds, my load weighed thirty.

The walking was rough, too, across rocky canyons and up and down steep ridges from one creek to the next. But we had been in the bush long enough now that we had hardened to the work of packing, and we struck out right after breakfast, never doubting that we'd make the fourteen miles to Cabin No. 3 well before dark. Two miles short of our destination, bad luck overtook us.

We found our way blocked by a narrow gorge, with rock walls too sheer to be climbed, and one of the mishaps Olive and Vala had worried about occurred.

We had to get across the gorge if we could, for there was no way of knowing how far we'd have to walk to get around it. John searched and found a narrow ledge leading down almost to the bottom, crossing in the form of a crack in a big outcrop and angling up to the top of the far side. It looked as if some tremen-

188

dous natural force or pressure had split the rock at some time in the distant past, leaving this sloping shelf.

It was narrow and treacherous, but it afforded a footpath of sorts. John tested it and decided we could walk it if we were very careful how and where we placed our feet.

We had a length of rope along. Each of us tied an end of it around his waist, roping us together after the fashion of mountain climbers, and John went ahead. When he was safely across I started after him.

I have always been frightened and unsteady in high places, and it was something I didn't want to do, but there wasn't much choice.

"Don't look down," John cautioned me. He knew I could rarely cross a log over a creek without falling off. "Just keep your eyes fixed straight ahead."

I made it down to the bottom and started up the far side. I had only a few more steps to go to reach level ground when the ax I was carrying caught on some obstruction and threw me off balance. I pitched off the ledge headfirst.

There was a small cuplike hollow directly below me, and I didn't have more than ten or a dozen feet to fall. But the hollow was floored with broken rock, and I'd almost certainly have been seriously injured or killed had it not been for John and the rope.

He had taken up the slack as I inched along the rock shelf. Now he tightened it with a hard tug, turning me right side up in the air. I landed on my feet. But I crumpled down in a heap, and when I tried to stand, my left foot would not bear my weight. I had twisted it severely, and my side hurt as if I had also cracked a couple of ribs.

I howled with pain. Then I heard John calling down to ask how badly I was hurt.

"I don't know," I sobbed.

But after a while I managed to get to my feet. I picked up the rifle I had been carrying and examined it to see whether it had been damaged. It looked to be in better shape than I was.

"Untie your rope," John instructed me, "and tie your packboard and the ax and gun on it so I can haul 'em up. Then I'll pull you up."

I sent my load up as he told me, and then the end of the rope came snaking back down to me, and it was my turn. The way my ribs were hurting I dreaded the thought of it, but there was no other way to get to the top. I knotted the rope securely around my body under the arms, and for safety's sake John made his end fast around a protruding rock. Then he started to haul me up, hand over hand.

My husband weighed 227 pounds that summer. My weight was 117. He made easy work of it and was as gentle as he could be. Even so, I groaned and screamed with pain.

When he had me safe at the top, he found a spot where there was soft moss on the ground, helped me to it, and eased me down.

"Sick at your stomach?" he asked gently,

I shook my head. "Why are you asking that?"

"That's likely to be a sign of a broken bone," he explained. "I don't think you have any. You sprained your ankle and got shook up inside, but it could be a lot worse."

The shame I felt at hurting myself in this far-off place and the thought of all the trouble I was causing were almost as hard to bear as the hurt itself. But I held back my tears. They would do no good, and I knew that John disliked to see a woman sniveling. I even managed a weak smile to let him know how much I appreciated the consideration he was showing me.

When I could stand he cut me a short green stick for a cane. He shouldered my pack on top of his, and I undertook to walk. The best I could do was hobble, and every step was pure agony. We covered less than a half mile, with the pain growing worse and worse, and John called a halt.

"We'll leave the packs, and I'll come back for them," he said. "I'll take you piggyback the rest of the way."

We got to Cabin No. 3 about four o'clock that afternoon. At the edge of the little clearing, John pulled up short.

"What the hell now?" he burst out.

The door was torn half off, hanging lopsided by its top hinge. The one window had been broken out, and through the open door we could see that the inside of the place was a shambles.

"White-Ear again," I mumbled.

"White-Ear or another one like him," John agreed.

He set me down on a block of wood and walked inside to look things over. He walked gingerly, too, and I was keeping a sharp watch all around, for we had left our rifles back with the packs.

The pole table and the pole bunk inside the cabin had been demolished and scattered over the dirt floor. The stove was cuffed aside, and a box of food supplies had been smashed and shoved through the window. We had left a cache of dried fish and meat hanging from the ridge pole. Everything had been torn down and either eaten or strewn about. The bear had done a thorough job of ruining things, as they almost unfailingly do when they invade a camp.

We had eaten nothing since breakfast, and we were hungry from the long hike and all that had happened. John had a few fishhooks in his hatband and a fish line in a back pocket. He went out on the lake and in a few minutes he had enough Dolly Vardens for our supper.

We didn't even wait to repair the stove. We built a small fire outside the cabin and roasted the fish on green sticks. "I could have eaten mine raw if I'd had to," I told John.

When we finished the meal, he nailed the cabin door securely back in place, stuffed gunnysacks into the broken window frame, fixed up the stove, and then started back after our packs. I was left alone without a gun and with a crippled ankle, and I waited in dread every minute he was gone, expecting and fearing the grizzly's return. But nothing happened.

John brought both packs in one trip. It was close to dark when he got back, and he was tired enough that he fell asleep the minute he turned in. But my ribs and ankles let me get very little sleep that night.

I was not hurt as severely as I had thought, however. My injuries healed quickly, and in a couple of weeks I was as good as new and ready for the trail once more. In the meantime, I had limped around the cabin and done my share of the camp chores.

John put in the time prospecting and panning on small gravel-bottom creeks that ran into End Lake. Two or three mornings after my fall he headed out right after breakfast, leaving me resting on the pole bed.

Shortly after he left I noticed that he had overlooked taking his rifle along. That worried me, for this was an area that seemed to crawl with grizzlies, and we were sure that White-Ear was still lurking somewhere in the neighborhood and that he still had a chip on his shoulder.

John had been gone about three hours when I heard a noise I couldn't quite make out. At first it sounded like two trees groaning against one another in the wind. I raised up on the bed to listen, and when it came again it sounded more like a human yell.

I cocked my ears and waited for what seemed like minutes. Probably it wasn't five seconds. Then, loud and distinct, I heard a shout for help and recognized John's voice.

I bounded off the bed, grabbed up my .30-30, and hopped to the door on one foot, hardly thinking about my sore ankle. When I swung the door open I saw John coming across an open place along the lake shore, with a big grizzly in hot pursuit only yards behind him.

John saw me in the doorway and swerved toward the lake to give me a clear shot. I got the bear in my sights and squeezed off.

The grizzly grunted like a pig, spun, and bit himself on a hind leg, and I knew I had hit him there.

John had his knife out now. He reached the lake and went off the bank in a headlong dive. I shot again but missed, and the bear turned and ran. John swam ashore, holding the knife in his teeth, and walked up the bank, looking for a dead bear. There was no dead bear to be found.

We learned weeks later that I had inflicted only a shallow wound. My bullet had sliced through the fleshy part of the hind leg just under the skin, cutting a deep gash and drawing considerable blood but doing no real damage. By the time we finally settled accounts with the bear, the wound was almost healed.

John came into the cabin, got his rifle, and took the blood trail. Despite the fact that it led off into thick brush, he followed it until the blood sign petered out. This was a grizzly that had to be killed if possible. As long as he roamed the area, neither our camps nor we would be safe, and now that he had been shot at and hit, he'd be more dangerous than ever.

John was gone two hours. When he finally lost the track, the bear was still traveling in a straight line for the high Wolverines.

John sat down and told me what had happened. He had finished panning in a tiny creek only a hundred yards from camp, and looked up, ready to climb out on the bank. The grizzly was standing about thirty yards away, watching him intently. The first thing John noticed was that he had one white ear.

John started to move away, hoping to widen the distance between them, but the instant he moved, the bear came in a businesslike rush. It was not more than two or three jumps behind him when I shot and certainly would have overtaken him before he could have made it to either the lake or the cabin.

As soon as my ankle was well enough, we shouldered our packs once more and headed for the Osilinka River, where John thought our chances would be the best of the summer.

He was proven right, too. We averaged eight ounces of gold a day there for several days and at thirty-five dollars an ounce, the price we expected to get, we counted that a good haul.

We had pitched our tent on the bank of the river not far upstream from where it ran into the Omineca. It was a good campsite, but I confess I missed the comforts of the old cabins. There were grizzlies here, too, and I also missed the feeling of safety that came from having four walls around me at night, even if they were flimsy walls laid up long ago of small poles.

Another prospector came along one day, a grizzled old-timer who introduced himself as Ernie Pitts. He ate supper with us, and while we sat around the fire afterward, the talk turned from gold panning to bears.

"I had a real go-around with a big grizzly this last spring," Ernie told us. "He damn near got me.

"I've got a cabin back toward the mountains a ways, and I wintered in it. As soon as the ice went out and the creeks opened up I started panning. I wasn't half a mile from the cabin one morning when I spotted this grizzly in the brush ahead, walking to meet me. I turned and ran, and he came for me like a barnyard bull."

Ernie climbed the first tree he came to that was big enough, he related. It was a small pine, but it put him beyond the bear's reach, and he figured he was safe. Like many people living in bear country, he believed that the grizzly cannot climb. That isn't quite true.

As a rule, this bear makes no effort to go up a tree, maybe because its front claws are too long for climbing in the way the black bear does, and the human who takes refuge in a tree is safe enough. But there are a few cases on record where an infuriated-grizzly's victim took to a tree with thick branches growing all the way to the ground, and the bear climbed about as readily as a man going up a ladder, sometimes high enough to bend the tree with its weight.

The bear that was chasing Pitts did not try to do that. Instead, it did something that John and I had never heard of before. It stood erect on its hind legs, hooked its front feet into the low branches of the pine, and tried deliberately to shake the man out.

"He shook that tree until he loosened the roots in the ground and it started to lean," the old prospector declared. "I had my arms and knees locked around the trunk halfway to the top, and it was all I could do to hang on."

At that point a cow moose appeared at the edge of the brush, tagged by a young calf. She heard the growling of the grizzly and the racket it was making, and she and the calf ran for cover. But the bear had seen them and took off after them. Pitts waited until he was sure it was not coming back, he told us. Then he climbed down and ran for his cabin as fast as his legs would carry him.

"Funny thing about that bear," he concluded. "He had one white ear. I never seen another like him."

John and I exchanged glances. There was no chance that the man was embellishing the story for our benefit, for up to that point we had made no mention of the white-eared grizzly. And somehow neither of us was too surprised. The ending of the story struck us as entirely logical. If any bear in the area was going to do what that one had done, it would be White-Ear.

"We've been running across him all summer," John said, and then he went on to relate the story of our encounters.

One afternoon a few days later, John cut himself a slim young aspen for a fish pole and walked down to the river to catch our supper, while I was busy around the fire. I was inside the tent when I heard a sudden splash and a loud whoop. My mind screamed "Bear!" and I grabbed up my rifle and ran outside.

I still laugh when I recall the scene. John was in the river up to his neck, trying vainly to climb the slippery bank. He was hanging grimly to his pole with one hand, and it was plain that something on the other end was doing its best to take the pole away from him.

The something turned out to be a rainbow trout that weighed twelve pounds, fast as lightning and hard as nails. Out on shore, John could have handled him with ease, but neck-deep in the river it was a different matter. He had lost his footing on the bank and gone into the water when the fish made its first rush. He kept grabbing overhanging brush with his free hand, but he wouldn't let go of the pole, and time after time the trout pulled him off balance and he lost his grip on the brush.

Finally I laid my gun down, found a pole, pushed one end out to him, and hooked my free arm around a tree. Between us we pulled him up on shore, and then he had no trouble landing the trout.

Toward the end of August we made a trip by boat up the Ingenika River and crossed trails with another picturesque old-timer, a bush trapper and prospector who was hiking back to his cabin at the foot of Pelly Mountain.

He was wearing Indian moccasins and carrying a small pack, traveling at a fast walk along the riverbank when we first saw him.

"They call me Caribou John," he said when John asked his name. Around the supper fire that night, we learned that his full name was John Bolderson.

He was a nervous, excitable man, between fifty and sixty years old, sturdily built but quick in all his motions. His hair, sprinkled with white, hadn't been cut for a month or two, and he was wearing a week's stubble of grayish beard, but his clothes were neat and clean. His English carried a pleasant flavor of another language, and we enjoyed talking with him.

We spent the rest of the afternoon with him and camped with

him that night. What followed had to be sheer coincidence, and hard to believe, but I'll take oath it happened.

Caribou John had just made a trip out to Fort Grahame and come back with a supply of tobacco and a grubstake for the winter, he told us, and he had a bear story to relate.

Carrying a heavy pack load of supplies from his boat up to his cabin only a few days before, he had come face to face with a big grizzly. He had no gun along since his hands were full with the packing job. He stopped, and he and the bear stared at each other through a screen of brush, only a few yards apart.

"That damn bear wasn't any more afraid of me than I am of a rabbit," Caribou John said.

He had hung his jacket on a bush at the side of the trail earlier because the day was warm. Grizzly and man stood their ground and tried to stare each other down for maybe two or three minutes. Then the bear made a sudden lunge, not for the trapper but for the jacket, grabbed it, and ran. Its owner found it a couple of days later, half buried in leaves and litter, up the hill behind his cabin.

He had not seen enough of the bear's head to know whether it had a patch of white, but when he finished his story, John and I would have given odds that he had run across White-Ear.

Caribou John's rifle was a relic, an old British .303 not worth the powder to blow it up, as my husband said. The barrel had a bulge, probably as a result of being fired at some time in the past when the muzzle was plugged with dirt or snow. I tested the gun by shoving one of its bullets into the muzzle, and the bullet fitted so loosely it wobbled. John and I tried to tell the man that he couldn't hit the door of his cabin with it at thirty yards, and if he risked using it on a grizzly, he'd almost certainly get into trouble.

But Caribou John had carried that rifle for many years and felt a real affection for it. He wouldn't listen to our advice. When my husband talked about the danger of wounding a grizzly at close range, he jumped to his feet and stomped around. "By damn, you just let that bear come within four hundred feet of me when I've got my gun and I'll blow his brains out!" he yelled.

He was to get the chance far sooner than any of us expected. We slept in the open that night, with no tent. Caribou John made himself a bed of soft spruce branches and arranged his pack for a pillow.

John and I went down to the creek fishing shortly before dark. The fishing was good, and when we started back I had seven trout in my pack, weighing around two and a half pounds apiece. Halfway to camp I saw something move and caught a glimpse of the rump of a brown-colored bear running off through the brush.

I had a strong hunch that White-Ear had located us once more, and John shared my opinion. If we were right, we could expect trouble. When it came time to turn in, he and I agreed that it would be wise to take turns and keep watch through the night. If this was the white-eared grizzly, he wouldn't hesitate to raid us for our fish or whatever he wanted, and we didn't want to be taken by surprise in the dark.

I picked the first half of the night. I'd stay awake until midnight, then I'd arouse John and he would take over until morning.

Nothing happened on my shift. When I shook John awake, he no longer thought it necessary to stand watch. "If that had been White-Ear you saw, we'd have heard more from him before this," he told me.

We slept soundly until dawn, but just as the first daylight was breaking, John shook my shoulder and whispered, "I can hear something heavy coming down the creek."

He and I were on our feet in seconds, with our rifles ready. Caribou John heard the commotion, and he jumped up and joined us.

The movement in the brush stopped, and for minutes the daybreak stillness was unbroken. Then we heard a noise off to one side, away from the creek.

"He's circling camp," John said in a low undertone.

"That's a bear," Caribou John blurted. "That's a grizzly."

John motioned him to silence, and we went on watching and waiting.

The next half hour seemed to last half a day. The light brightened slowly and we could see into the brush, but nothing stirred. The trapper lay down on his spruce-bough bed again and seemed to be dozing off. Then, without warning, a big bear stepped into the open, at a point exactly opposite the place where we had last heard him. He had made a half circle around our camp without rustling a leaf.

He stopped just clear of the brush, swung his head, and sniffed in the direction where we had hung our trout from the low branch of a tree. Neither John nor I were surprised in the least that he had a white patch around one ear.

If Caribou John had really dozed off, he was a light sleeper. He was on his feet in a second, and he and John shot almost together. I saw a twig clipped over the bear's back and mentally blamed it on the bulged .303. Then the trapper blasted out two more shots in quick succession, and yelled, "I got him! I got him!"

The grizzly answered instantly with a roar of rage that sent shivers up my back. Somebody once said that a man will live ten years longer if he never hears a big bear bawl in anger. I must say I know of no other sound that matches it.

The next thing I saw was White-Ear running straight for Caribou John. The trapper was standing off to one side, and the bear had its eyes fixed on him and its mind made up. If it saw John and me, it gave no sign.

John was between me and the bear, and I didn't get a chance to shoot. Maybe that was just as well. My .30-30 was hardly adequate for this job. But John's .30/06 bellered twice, and the grizzly stopped, whipped his head angrily from side to side, and bit at his ribs. Then he stood, bawling, clawing brush and dry leaves in every direction.

Caribou John had had only six or seven shells to begin with. His rifle was empty now, but he was hopping up and down, yelling, "I got him! I plugged him!"

John shot again, and the bear went down. He was still thrashing and bawling and tearing up the ground. We waited until he dragged himself clear of the brush, then John walked a few steps closer and finished him with a shot in the head.

The grizzly that had plagued us throughout the summer was finally disposed of. John's first shot had hit him in the chest, the second had gone through his side a little too far back, the third had smashed into his neck close to the spine. That was the one that disabled him. There was no evidence that Caribou John had inflicted any damage. But the trapper still thought he had done the killing, and we made no attempt to disillusion him.

When we looked the bear over we found the wound I had left in his hind leg the day John jumped into End Lake to escape him. It was almost healed now and plainly had not been much of a handicap. If it had done anything, in all likelihood it had increased his hatred for humans and made him more short-tempered than ever.

There were other things about him that probably had helped to account for his readiness to pick a fight, too. He was an old bear, in very poor condition, long legged but gaunt and skinny looking. His teeth were worn down and broken, and it seemed evident that he had gone hungry most of the time for at least the last year or two of his life. No wonder he had had a chip on his shoulder and was ready to attack anything that came near him. As John remarked, a hungry bear is always a bear to watch out for.

We'd have liked to keep his pelt, for he was a big grizzly and the white ear patch made him highly unusual. But we had no way to salvage the hide. We had killed him too far from any of our cabins, and we did not have enough salt with us to preserve the pelt. On top of that, green and undried, it would be a very heavy load to pack out. We left him where we had killed him, unskinned.

We went on to Caribou John's cabin with him that day, on foot, had an excellent supper of smoked trout, and spent the night there. Then we hiked back to our boat and began our return trip out of the area.

October came, stripping the aspens of their yellow leaves and bringing freezing nights. It was time to start back to civilization.

We decided against retracing our steps and going home the way we had come north in the spring, through McLeod Lake and Summit Lake to Prince George. Instead, we'd go down the Omineca and the Finlay to the Peace at Finlay Forks, and there, rather than follow the Parsnip upstream to McLeod, we'd let the current of the mighty Peace carry us down to the town of Peace River Crossing. From there we could take a train to Edmonton. We were tired of poling and portaging and packing. It would be good for a change to sit back and let the river and our motor do all the work.

I was almost as eager now to get out of the bush as I had been eager to lose ourselves in it back in May. I was beginning to be haunted by visions of mashed potatoes and brown gravy and big slabs of apple pie with ice cream on the side.

We had traveled only a few miles on the Peace when two men appeared on shore and waved us in. They told us they had been panning for a month at the mouths of creeks running into the river. They knew the Peace well and asked if we had ever run it. When we said no, they drew a crude map in the sand indicating where we would find bad rapids.

We camped there with them that night, and while we were

talking by the dead fire after supper a calf moose ran out of the willow bottoms not thirty yards from where we sat. Then two big wolves came racing after it.

The calf saw us, turned, and ran back into the brush with the wolves close on its heels, and then we heard a thrashing and a loud wailing bleat. One of the prospectors headed for their tent for his rifle, but John and I were ahead of him. We grabbed up our guns and ran for the commotion.

John was about three jumps ahead of me. At the edge of the brush he held up a hand to warn me to silence. Then his .30/06 cracked out two whiplash reports, so close together that they blurred into one. When I overtook him he was looking down at a dead wolf, and a few yards away the moose calf lay hamstrung, struggling to get back on its feet. The second wolf had made a getaway.

"Damn that pair!" John said fervently.

He put the calf out of its misery, and we started back the way it and the wolves had come. Five hundred yards back we found the mother, down on her hind quarters, hamstrung like the youngster, her back legs as useless as if they had been cut off. In hamstringing, incidentally, wolves do not necessarily sever the main tendon of the leg. They need only to slash at it and mangle it to do enough damage that it will not support the weight of the animal attacked.

There were no other injuries on the cow moose. The wolves had gone on after the calf the instant she was disabled, without bothering to tear at her. Had we not found and killed her, she would have been doomed to lie for two or three days and die a lingering death. Once more I had been given good reason for my undying hatred of all wolves.

At Portage Mountain Canyon on the Peace, we hit our first bad water, a stretch of rapids fourteen miles long, too rough for our boat. We hired a man with a team and wagon, loaded everything, and he portaged us around. The rest of the way to Peace River Crossing we made good time. And at last my dream meal became a reality.

"It's surprising how you can crave pie and ice cream," I told John that evening.

At Edmonton we sold our gold at the government price of $35 an ounce. We had ninety ounces to sell, and it yielded us more than $3,200 for our summer of work and fun.

That was more money than I had seen at one time in all my forty-six years.

Epilogue

There is not a great deal more to tell.

Not long after our summer of gold panning, John and I bought a sawmill near Prince George. We operated it until we tired of sawmilling, then we went back to the Stuart and purchased the Jack Hamilton place near my old homestead, where I had gone for mail the day the she bear chased me, so many years before.

We built a new house and bought some livestock. Then John decided to start a logging operation upriver, floating the logs down to our place in booms of four hundred, through the same reaches where I had hunted moose from a dugout as a young widow. We set up another sawmill, hauling the sawed lumber to town by truck.

John was away from home much of the time, and I was left by myself to run the ranch, look after our sheep and the herd of whiteface cattle that were our special pride, and market chickens, eggs, beef, and potatoes in town.

Some of the chores were hard, in more ways than one. I had a heifer calf five months old that I had named Velvet and raised as a pet. Without warning, something went wrong with her. She stopped eating for a day or two at a time and bloated badly. Then she'd recover and be okay for a day or two, only to fall sick again.

I was used to handling and doctoring animals, and I tried all the usual medicines, but nothing effected a cure. The situation went on for days, and finally she bloated so badly that I decided to tap her by perforating her paunch through the side. Farmers and ranchers at that time often resorted to that in extreme cases. It was a drastic procedure, done with a sharp knife, but it brought immediate relief to a bloated animal and sometimes saved its life.

I performed the operation on Velvet and inserted a rubber tube in the puncture wound. That worked well for the better part of two days, then the tube plugged and I had to take it out, clean it, and insert it again. I had to work single-handed, and the job proved no easy one for a woman handling a five-month-old calf by herself.

John came home on one of his brief trips about that time, and we agreed that if the calf did not recover, she would have to be shot. That was something I really dreaded, but it was the only humane thing to do. When the time came, I held the muzzle of the .30-30 against her head, and she died with hardly a quiver.

I dressed her out for dog food, and when I opened her paunch the cause of the trouble was plain. A ball of oakum, the size of a man's fist, was knotted in the stomach. Oakum is a tarry material that resembles shredded rope.

Now I confronted another problem. Where had the oakum come from? I had to find it or expect to lose more cattle.

The search proved easier than I anticipated. There was an old tumble-down log cabin in the middle of the pasture. I checked and discovered that at some time in the past it had been partly chinked with the stuff. The calf had pulled out a few bites from between the crumbling logs, probably liking the taste of tar, and swallowed it, signing her own death warrant.

I fenced the cabin off to keep the rest of the cattle away and had no more trouble.

The combination of logging, sawmilling, and ranching brought us a good income but was very hard work for both of us. We kept it up for five years, and then it became too much to handle. We eased off the load, doing nothing in winter except feeding and caring for our livestock. In summer, when the cattle and sheep were at pasture, we put in the time fishing and driving to the end of every back road we could find, to see what there was to look at. Whichever way we went there was plenty—lakes and rivers and creeks, mountains and valleys and wild meadows.

In 1962 we sold the ranch and moved to a home in Vanderhoof. We lived comfortably there for six years, going on long fishing and camping trips in summer, hunting moose and deer each fall.

In the spring of 1968, hoping to find relief from the increasingly severe discomfort of arthritis, we sold our Vanderhoof home and moved once more, this time to the village of Okanagan Falls south of Lake Okanagan, in British Columbia, twenty-five miles north of the United States border. That is where we are living as this story comes to an end.

As for my two daughters, Olive had had more than her share of misfortune and grief. Her first husband, Alex Dome, was killed near Montreal in the crash of a bomber he was test-flying in February of 1943. She married Fred Giguere, another airline captain, in 1945. He died in 1962 in a crash at Honolulu. My twice-widowed daughter married her third husband, Larry Allen, two years later. She now has five children, the two boys from her first marriage and three girls, and she and Larry live at Pemberton, British Columbia, where he and his brother own and operate a hotel business.

Vala has been more fortunate. She took nurse's training, and married Gordon Magnant in the fall of 1949, when she was twenty-six. Gordon owns and drives a logging truck, working out of Prince George. They have one son, and live a few miles south of there.

For the most part I have talked here of things that happened a long time ago. My life since John and I were married has been a happy one, filled with work and enjoyment, but neither eventful nor turbulent.

The changes that have come to the wild country I knew are hard to believe. A paved highway runs north now from Prince George to Summit Lake and McLeod Lake, where John and I traveled by riverboat and where we said good-bye to civilization in the summer of 1948.

A gravel road goes north from Vanderhoof past Fort St. James and angles on into the mountain country to Germansen Landing, and then north another forty or fifty miles to Tutizzi Lake. But beyond that, I'm happy to say, there is still roadless wilderness in the Omineca Mountains, and north for another two hundred miles through the Stikines, the Skeena range, and the Cassiars to Watson Lake on the Alaska Highway. This is still mountain sheep and grizzly country, remote and unspoiled. Fort Ware and Fort Grahame still get their freight by boat. One of the biggest changes of all has been wrought by the Bennett Dam on the Peace, which has created a huge and sprawling impoundment, Williston Lake, in the Finlay Forks area. The lake, shaped like an upside-down **Y**, stretches north and south for some one hundred and fifty miles and has left much of the country we knew there under water.

I am a woman past seventy now, and the final years of my life are not proving too kind. I am plagued with severe arthritis, and I am going blind from glaucoma. Doctors tell me the total loss of my sight is almost inevitable. It may come gradually or suddenly, but it is almost sure to come. The idea of blindness is hard to face, but I have had enough misfortune in my lifetime to teach me to resign myself to what must be. Above all, I do not feel that I have any reason to complain.

Much of my life has been hard. The winter and spring on the trapline with Walter were an ordeal almost too terrible to be endured, and those early years at the homestead on the Stuart, when my three children were small, were an endless grind of toil and hardship. But it all turned out better than I dared to hope, and if there is any greater satisfaction in life than hard work done for a worthwhile purpose and obstacles overcome that seem too formidable to surmount, I have not found it and do not know what it is.

And if much of my life has been hard, it was also wonderful. I can cry with the Welsh miner, how green were my valleys, how white my winter woods!

I have such a host of splendid memories. The fast water of big north-country rivers, the awesome roar of ice-out, the feel of a canoe in quiet current. The lush wild-hay meadows along the Athabasca, the late-summer thickets hanging heavy with wild fruit, the color of gold in a pan. The warmth and comfort of a chinked cabin, a wood fire crackling in a tiny stove, the whisper of dogsled runners on frozen snow.

Most of all, I think, I like to recall the stillness of the north and revel in the recollection. The windless nights of winter, cold and clear, when the white radiance of the moon was beauty to take your breath away. The days when the sun shone blindingly bright in a cloudless sky, or when snow sifted to earth as silently as floating thistledown.

There is a quiet over the northern wilderness at such times, a silence so complete it can be felt, a peace that bids the spirit soar. I hope I never forget an hour of the times when I have known that stillness to lay its spell on the land.

As for the hardships and privations that were once my lot, I had a wonderful letter not long ago from a woman I have never met, and in all likelihood never shall, since she lives in a Midwestern state a thousand miles from me. It was a letter to warm the heart.

"You are a plucky woman," she wrote, "with character and courage. There is urgent need in the world today for more like you. I hope you are grateful to God for the grit that saw you through, and for the appreciation and wonder you have felt all your life for the earth and its places of wildness and beauty and solitude."

I am grateful to God indeed!